FRANCIS FRITH'S

HEMEL HEMPSTEAD - A HISTORY & CELEBRATION

THE FRANCIS FRITH COLLECTION

www.francisfrith.com

HEMEL HEMPSTEAD

A HISTORY & CELEBRATION

ELIZABETH BUTEUX

THE FRANCIS FRITH COLLECTION

www.francisfrith.com

First published in the United Kingdom in 2005
by The Francis Frith Collection®

Hardback Edition 2005 ISBN 1-84589-206-2
Paperback Edition 2011 ISBN 978-1-84589-591-4

British Library Cataloguing in Publication Data

Hemel Hempstead - A History & Celebration
Elizabeth Buteux

The Francis Frith Collection
Oakley Business Park, Wylye Road,
Dinton, Wiltshire SP3 5EU
Tel: +44 (0) 1722 716 376
Email: info@francisfrith.co.uk
www.francisfrith.com

Printed and bound in England

Front Cover: **HEMEL HEMPSTEAD, THE TOWN HALL, LOOKING
SOUTH c1890** ZZZ03350t (Dacorum Heritage Trust Ltd)

Additional modern photographs by Peter Grainger.

Domesday extract used in timeline by kind permission of
Alecto Historical Editions, www.domesdaybook.org
Aerial photographs reproduced under licence from
Simmons Aerofilms Limited.
Historical Ordnance Survey maps reproduced under licence from
Homecheck.co.uk

Every attempt has been made to contact copyright holders of
illustrative material. We will be happy to give full acknowledgement in future
editions for any items not credited. Any information should be directed to
The Francis Frith Collection.

*The colour-tinting in this book is for illustrative purposes only,
and is not intended to be historically accurate*

CONTENTS

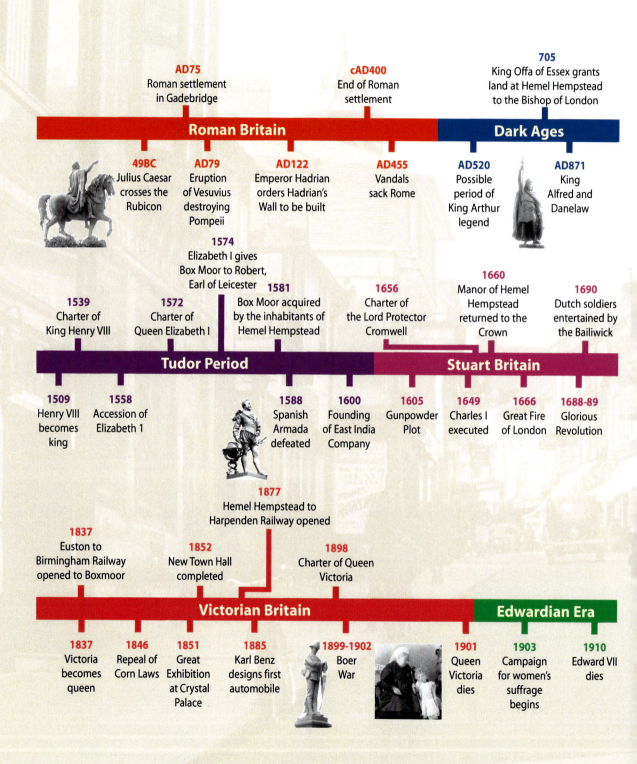

AD75 Roman settlement in Gadebridge

cAD400 End of Roman settlement

705 King Offa of Essex grants land at Hemel Hempstead to the Bishop of London

Roman Britain

Dark Ages

49BC Julius Caesar crosses the Rubicon

AD79 Eruption of Vesuvius destroying Pompeii

AD122 Emperor Hadrian orders Hadrian's Wall to be built

AD455 Vandals sack Rome

AD520 Possible period of King Arthur legend

AD871 King Alfred and Danelaw

1574 Elizabeth I gives Box Moor to Robert, Earl of Leicester

1581 Box Moor acquired by the inhabitants of Hemel Hempstead

1660 Manor of Hemel Hempstead returned to the Crown

1690 Dutch soldiers entertained by the Bailiwick

1539 Charter of King Henry VIII

1572 Charter of Queen Elizabeth I

1656 Charter of the Lord Protector Cromwell

Tudor Period

Stuart Britain

1509 Henry VIII becomes king

1558 Accession of Elizabeth 1

1588 Spanish Armada defeated

1600 Founding of East India Company

1605 Gunpowder Plot

1649 Charles I executed

1666 Great Fire of London

1688-89 Glorious Revolution

1877 Hemel Hempstead to Harpenden Railway opened

1837 Euston to Birmingham Railway opened to Boxmoor

1852 New Town Hall completed

1898 Charter of Queen Victoria

Victorian Britain

Edwardian Era

1837 Victoria becomes queen

1846 Repeal of Corn Laws

1851 Great Exhibition at Crystal Palace

1885 Karl Benz designs first automobile

1899-1902 Boer War

1901 Queen Victoria dies

1903 Campaign for women's suffrage begins

1910 Edward VII dies

HISTORICAL TIMELINE FOR HEMEL HEMPSTEAD

1066
Under Norman rule, Hemel Hempstead created a Manor held by Robert, the Count of Mortain

1086
Hemel Hempstead 'rated in ten hides' in the Domesday Book

1180
Completion of St Mary's Church

1290
Hemel Hempstead ruled by the Bonhommes at Ashridge Monastery

1360
Probable date of the Albyn brasses

Middle Ages | Late Medieval

1066
Battle of Hastings. Norman rule begins

1086
Domesday Book

1170
Murder of Thomas à Becket at Canterbury cathedral

1215
Magna Carta

1306
Robert the Bruce declares himself King of Scotland

1348
Black Death kills 25 million in Europe

1415
Battle of Agincourt

1485
Battle of Bosworth Field marks end of Plantaganet dynasty

1797
Trustees of Box Moor sell land to the Grand Junction Canal Company

1809
John Dickinson acquires Apsley Mill

1811
John Dickinson acquires Nash Mill

1802
Execution of the highwayman, Robert Snooks, on Box Moor

1809
Box Moor Trust Act regulates grazing

1827
The infirmary at Piccotts End established

c1725
High Street rebuilt

1749
Fire in the Market House

1762
The London Road turnpiked

Georgian Era

1739
John Wesley founds Methodist church

1762
Mozart performs at the age of 6

1789
French Revolution

1815
Battle of Waterloo

1825
Stockton to Darlington Railway

1997
Hemel Hempstead celebrates its 50th year as a New Town

1974
Local government reorganisation. The new authority is Dacorum District Council

1984
Charter of Elizabeth II. Dacorum granted borough status

1946
Hemel Hempstead selected to be a New Town

1952
Queen Elizabeth II visits Adeyfield

1966
Council move to the new civic centre

20th Century Britain

1914
First World War begins

1926
John Logie Baird obtains first television picture

1939
Outbreak of Second World War

1956
Suez Crisis

1966
England win World Cup

1969
First man on the Moon

1982
Falklands Conflict

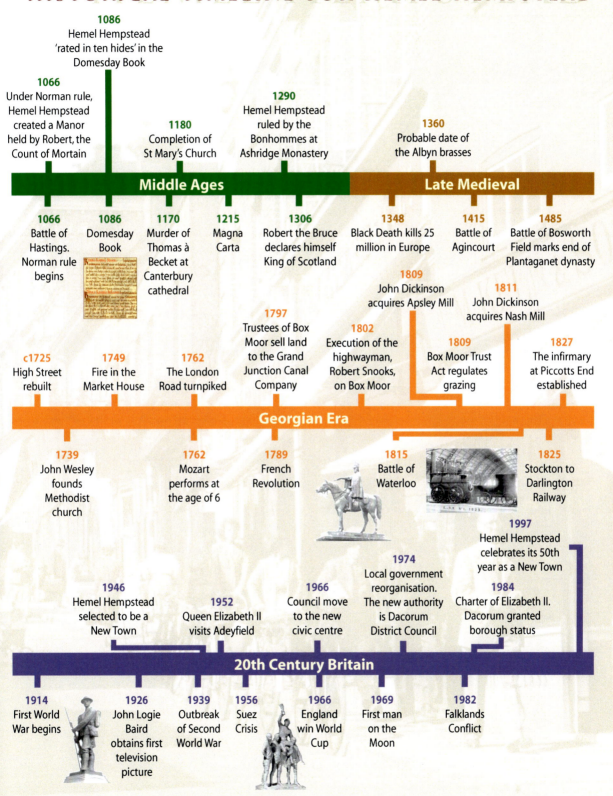

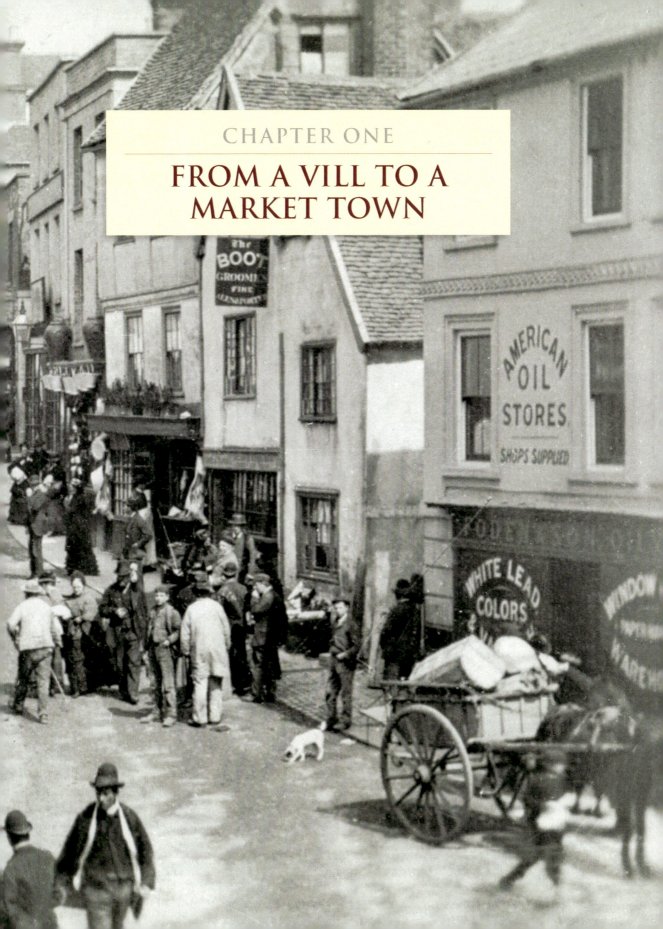

CHAPTER ONE

FROM A VILL TO A MARKET TOWN

HEMEL HEMPSTEAD, in Hertfordshire, is probably best known as a New Town, being built after the Second World War, but this overlooks its long and historic past.

Over the years there have been a variety of spellings of the name Hemel Hempstead. For instance, Hamaele is the Saxon name for the district of the early settlement, but by the 13th century the town was known as Hamelhamstede. Later, by the 17th century, the name had evolved as Hemelhemsted. From this time on, the name was sometimes shortened to Hemel or Hempstead. Even today, the town is often referred to as Hemel. The town now forms part of the Borough of Dacorum, a name of Danish origin.

Geographically Hemel Hempstead has a pleasant situation. It lies in the valleys of the Rivers Gade and Bulbourne, on the ridges of the Chiltern Hills only 25 miles from London. The town possesses two attractive and extensive open spaces; to the west of the old High Street lies Gadebridge Park, bought by the former Hemel Hempstead Borough Council in 1952; the second, further west, is Box Moor. Hemel Hempstead was, and indeed still is, geographically divided into three distinct parts. To the north is the old town of Hemel Hempstead, to the west lies Boxmoor, which derives its name from the moor, with Apsley established to the south. After the New Town was built, the three parts became closely linked by the neighbourhoods of Chaulden, Adeyfield, Bennets End, Gadebridge, Warners End, Grovehill and Highfield, together with the villages of Piccotts End and Leverstock Green. Yet to discover how all this came about we have to trace the town back to when it was a settlement in Roman times.

MARLOWES, HEMEL HEMPSTEAD 2005
H255701k (Peter Grainger)

HIGH STREET 1881 ZZZ03356 (Dacorum Heritage Trust Ltd)

Apart from the shop fronts the buildings remain mostly the same today. The American Oil Stores, however, seen at the corner, was replaced by Lloyds Bank in 1882.

CHAULDEN, THE SHOPPING CENTRE c1965 H255090

GADEBRIDGE PARK c1965 H255073

During the construction of the new Leighton Buzzard Road in 1963, the site of a Roman villa was found in Gadebridge Park. It was subsequently fully excavated between 1963 and 1968 by Dr David Neal, at that time being one of the most completely excavated villas in the country. The site was then sealed with protective materials before being re-covered. Dr Neal's findings revealed that the villa was begun about AD75 and was altered and expanded over a period of two and a half centuries. Between AD300 and AD325 a large bathing pool, only a little smaller than the famous pool at Bath, was constructed in addition to the already existing bathhouse. In the middle of the 4th century the house and the pool were demolished and eventually replaced by agricultural buildings.

We hear no more of our town until

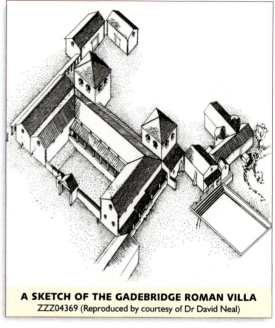

A SKETCH OF THE GADEBRIDGE ROMAN VILLA
ZZZ04369 (Reproduced by courtesy of Dr David Neal)

This illustration suggests what the villa may have looked like in AD325.

The first Roman finds made in the Hemel Hempstead area were in the burial ground of the Independent Chapel, Box Lane, in August and September 1837. Both were the remains of cremation burials. In 1850, Mr Byles, the stationmaster at Boxmoor station, found the remains of a Roman building and a well in his garden (now the car park of Hemel Hempstead station). Sir John Evans, the noted antiquarian, carried out the excavations on the two sites and a further excavation of a small house beside what is now Boxmoor House School.

AD705, when Offa, the King of Essex, granted land at Hamaele to the Bishop of London. Certainly the name 'Hamelhamstede', as the vill or village was called, is of Saxon origin. It clustered around the area that is now St Mary's Close, in the High Street, in the Old Town Centre.

At the time of the Norman Conquest, William the Conqueror ordered a survey of most of England so that he could see exactly what he owned. This document, the Domesday Book, was completed in 1086. It records that the relatively unimportant vill of Hamelhamstede, with about 100 inhabitants, was held by two brothers, the Earl of Leofwine's men. (Leofwine was a brother of King Harold who was killed at the Battle of Hastings.) The survey reveals that

Hemel Hempstead was 'rated in ten hides', a hide being approximately 100 acres. The document records 'pasture for cattle', and 'pannage for twelve hundred hogs'. There is also reference to four mills, foreshadowing the rich wheat-growing and cattle-producing area that Hemel Hempstead was to become.

One of the most important effects of the Norman Conquest was the reorganisation of landholding. Land was seized from Saxon owners and granted to Norman overlords. Hemel Hempstead then became a Manor, held by Robert, the Count of Mortain, William the Conqueror's elder half-brother. He held it as part of a great lordship in the area within his Honour of Berkhamsted. Thus the people of Hemel Hempstead lived under the shadow of Berkhamsted Castle. After the Count of Mortain, Hemel Hempstead was held by many royal lords, ladies and bishops including Thomas à Becket in 1162, Berengaria, queen of Richard I, and Isabella, the second wife of King John.

In 1290, King John's grandson, the Earl of Cornwall, gave the Manor of Hemel Hempstead to a group of monks called the Bonhommes and built a monastery for them at Ashridge. The Rector and the monks ruled Hemel Hempstead for 250 years. They drew the profits from the Manor and enjoyed the rectorial tithes. The mill at the Bury, which once stood at the end of the village, at what is now the junction of Queensway and Leighton Buzzard Road, was one of five mills granted to the monks in the area.

ST MARY'S CHURCH c1960 H255047

St Mary's Church, the parish church of Hemel Hempstead, stands to the west of the High Street, on a site running east to west. It is one of the best preserved of the Norman churches remaining in the country. The magnificent fluted leaden spire, which was added in the early 14th century, reaches 200 feet (61 m) to the gilded weather vane. It is reputed to be one of the highest church spires in Western Europe. Supporting it is the Norman central tower, rising in two clear stages and above the surrounding roofs.

The church was built of clunch (a soft white limestone) with some Roman brick and is cruciform in style. Begun in 1140, the church took 40 years to build and was dedicated to St Mary in 1150, when the chancel and tower were completed. The building of the nave and the west door followed; both are fine examples of decorated Norman architecture. In the nave the massive, but beautifully proportioned, arcades have sturdy round pillars with moulded bases and scalloped capitals, again showing expert Norman workmanship. Above the arcades are 12 clerestory windows; 11 of the original Norman windows have survived here. Two other Norman windows are also in existence, one in the chancel and another in the east wall of the south transept. The north and south aisles have 15th-century windows with 19th-century tracery, although the windowsills in the south aisle are Norman. At the back of the nave is the original font, but re-cut and embellished with biblical scenes in the 19th century.

ST MARY'S CHURCH 2005
H255702k (Peter Grainger)

The early history of St Mary's is difficult to trace as all documents relating to the parish were destroyed at the time of the Reformation. In a way it is a mystery how such a sumptuous church as St Mary's came to be built in the vill of Hemel Hempstead, especially as no Saxon church appears to have preceded it. According to some sources Reginald de Dunstanville was the builder of the church but this is probably not correct. There appears to be confusion between the role of the builder and that of the patron. In 1140, the same year that the building of the church commenced, King Stephen bestowed the earldom of Cornwall on Reginald de Dunstanville, a natural son of Henry I, and granted him Berkhamsted Castle. It is therefore very likely that Reginald de Dunstanville was the patron.

St Mary's provides us with a great deal of information about the people who lived in Hemel Hempstead. For example, we have to remember that the church was standing at the time of the Crusades, for on a pillar at the entrance to the chancel is graffiti. As the knights and soldiers left for the Holy Land they carved their initials or left marks on the stone. In this way they must have hoped that God would remember them and protect them.

At the back of the church are images of a knight and his lady. Standing against the west wall is a large slab removed from an altar tomb, bearing brass effigies of Robert Albyn and his wife, Margaret, who were local landowners. These date from the 14th century, probably 1360.

As we move on through the Middle Ages, we may well ask: 'What was life like for the people living in the vill of Hemel Hempstead?' Before the Reformation, peoples' lives were controlled by the single universal Catholic Church, so St Mary's would have been the centre of both religious and social life. However, the nave, which had no seating, belonged to the parishioners. It was not just a religious meeting-house but was used as a market and a corn exchange. The church ales were also held here, but the people were so rowdy that John Eggerton, the priest for St Mary's in 1527, strongly disapproved. The priest obtained permission from the Rector of Ashridge and the Bishop of Lincoln to build a Church House for social occasions. The parishioners also used the south porch, built in the 14th century, and the north

THE ALBYN BRASSES ZZZ04370 (Author's collection)

Fact File

The brasses are not a likeness of the Albyns. This style of brass was commonplace, being made in large numbers by London shops for stock, so they could be ordered ready-made. The iconography is relatively simple. As the dead man is a knight, his feet rest on a lion, symbolising courage. The lady's head rests on a cushion whilst the dog at her feet symbolises fidelity.

porch, added in the 15th century, to discuss parochial matters, and the expenditure of money. The original stained glass windows were used by the priest to teach an illiterate people the scriptures.

To the north of St Mary's, at Piccotts End, are cottages with medieval wall paintings which have been fully restored. Built in the late 15th century, it is thought that the buildings may have housed a hospice for pilgrims on their way to Ashridge. Over the years, Ashridge Monastery became a place of pilgrimage, for it housed a sacred relic of the blood of Christ authenticated by the Patriarch of Jerusalem. It was brought back from Jerusalem by Edmund, son of Richard, Earl of Cornwall in 1270. The drops were divided between Ashridge and Hailes Abbey, founded by the earl in 1251.

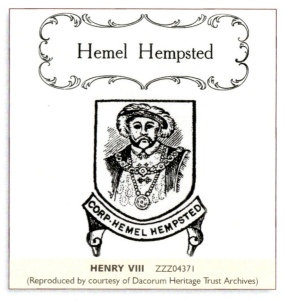

HENRY VIII ZZZ04371
(Reproduced by courtesy of Dacorum Heritage Trust Archives)

Henry VIII has become an emblem for Hemel Hempstead.

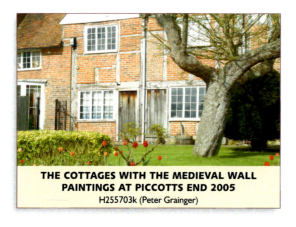

THE COTTAGES WITH THE MEDIEVAL WALL PAINTINGS AT PICCOTTS END 2005
H255703k (Peter Grainger)

After the Reformation, and with the suppression of Ashridge in 1539, the advowson of St Mary passed to the Dean and Chapter of St Paul's, London, who appointed a vicar on the nomination of the Bishop of Lincoln. However, it was not until the

accession of Edward VI, which brought many strict Protestants into high places, that images, saint worship, pilgrimages and processions were banned. In St Mary's the lights were put out and the subsidiary altars removed. In 1538, Thomas Cromwell had made the keeping of parish registers compulsory and these were stored at St Mary's in the 16th-century parish chest that faces the south door. There are many deaths recorded in the parish register referring to the plague that visited Hemel Hempstead in 1583 and 1593.

At the time of the Reformation Hemel Hempstead passed to the Crown, Henry VIII. In 1539, Hemel Hempstead received its Charter of Incorporation. This was granted by Henry VIII out of gratitude to his auditor, John Waterhouse, who had entertained the king with great splendour at his house, The Bury, in Hemel Hempstead.

The Charter Tower, which can be seen in Gadebridge Park behind the High Street is, according to popular belief, where Henry VIII presented the charter to the town. In fact the building is of a later date, and the former mansion, The Bury, where Henry stayed, was demolished in 1555. Before the Reformation it belonged to the last Rector of Ashridge, Thomas Waterhouse. In 1535, King Henry had granted it to Thomas's brother, John Waterhouse and his son-in-law, Richard Combe, who now, as Protestants, had changed religious sides. It was Sir Richard Combe who built the new Bury between 1557 and 1559, on the site of the earlier house, and the Charter Tower is the remaining porch of this new house. In 1791, The Bury was pulled down by Mr Ginger, a local attorney, who built himself an elegant house nearby, also called The Bury.

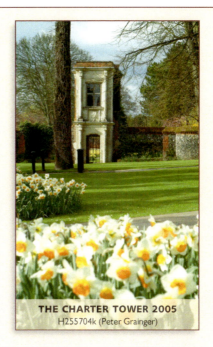

THE CHARTER TOWER 2005
H255704k (Peter Grainger)

THE BURY 2005 H255705k (Peter Grainger)

Standing at the entrance of Gadebridge Park, the house is now the Register Office.

Fact File

According to local legend, Henry VIII courted Anne Boleyn at Hemel Hempstead. However, when Henry visited John Waterhouse in 1539, it was for financial purposes. It certainly had nothing to do with Anne Boleyn, for she had been beheaded in 1536.

THOMAS WATERHOUSE ZZZ04372
(Author's collection)

Thomas Waterhouse, the last Rector of Ashridge, remained a Catholic, and is buried in the chancel of St Mary's Church.

NEW TOWN SHOPS c1960 H255012

When the New Town was being built many new streets were named after people linked with the town: King Harry Street, Waterhouse Street and Combe Street, are adjacent to Marlowes where the first new shops were constructed. However, King Henry would have been less than impressed to discover that Waterhouse Street is a fine street bordering the length of the Water Gardens, whereas the road bearing his name is a secondary road at the back of Marlowes.

The granting of the Royal Charter, on 29 December 1539, gave Hemel Hempstead the status of a Bailiwick, with the right to elect a Town Bailiff, and to hold an annual fair at the feast of Corpus Christi in June.

Most important of all was the right to hold a weekly market and to enjoy the ensuing profits. This was the seed from which the town's fortunes grew.

An eye-witness account confirms that a royal charter was vital to the growth and development of English towns. John Leland's 'Itinerary in England and Wales', begun in 1533 and finished in 1546,' records flourishing but unpretentious market towns, such as Berkhamsted, the nearest market for the people of Hemel Hempstead. By comparison Leland's only reference to Hemel Hempstead is the meeting of two rivers, the Gade and Bulbourne, at Two Waters. This was already an established settlement, and there was

THE WATER GARDENS c1960 H255043

The Water Gardens when they were first laid out. The new office building on the right, Stephens Chambers, was named after William Stephyns, in 1539 the first elected Bailiff of Hemel Hempstead.

sufficient water power to drive two corn mills, one at Two Waters itself and the other at nearby Frogmore End.

Today, Two Waters is the centre of an important new road layout. The M25 is only three miles away and a new improved A41 primary trunk route brings traffic to Two Waters and to within easy access to the entry of the town. Two Waters Road crosses the London Road, the old A41, and from the traffic lights the London Road leads to Apsley, and west to Hemel Hempstead railway station. When the London Road was turnpiked in 1726, the Bell Inn was an important coaching inn. It survived as a successful pub and restaurant until quite recently when it underwent a metamorphosis to become a McDonald's.

At the time of the charter there was no High Street. According to the 1523 Rental later, in 'Churchend' there were ten houses dotted around St Mary's Church. The ground where the market place was to be built was a ploughed field.

Another royal connection with Hemel Hempstead is of importance to its early development. After her arrest in 1554, Princess Elizabeth travelled along Cherry Bounce, a lane leading off the north of the High Street. She was on her way from Ashridge to London to answer charges of conspiracy to seize the throne. Four years later she became Elizabeth I and in 1572 she also granted a charter to the town. Although it was her father's charter that gave Hemel Hempstead the right to hold a market, it was Elizabeth's charter that stimulated its development. It gave St Mary's Church the tenure of royal land adjoining the churchyard that provided a site for a Market House and other buildings.

Market Street, as the High Street was known then, began to become established. However, it did not look as it does today, for at this time the buildings were not a continuous line. A study of the Bailiwick records shows that the street was narrow with unsanitary conditions. On either side were strips of wasteland on which stalls were erected for the markets and fairs. The market was a general one, but from the evidence of wills, wheat emerges as the main crop. There were already five mills in the district for grinding corn. Thus, Hemel Hempstead slowly evolved from a small Anglo-Saxon vill to a flourishing market town.

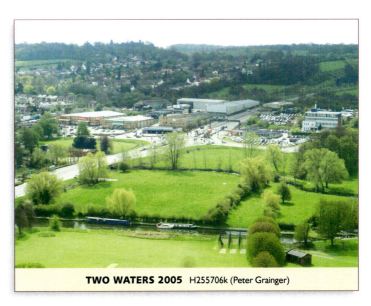

TWO WATERS 2005 H255706k (Peter Grainger)

CHAPTER TWO

AN 'EXTRAORDINARY CORN MARKET'

AS LONDON grew to become one of the major cities in Europe, Hemel Hempstead became one of the principal corn markets for London. Indeed, Daniel Defoe commented in his book on English towns, written in 1726, that 'The Town of Hempstead is noted for an extraordinary corn market.'

Although it was the corn market, with its status and reputation as the granary of London, that brought prosperity to Hemel Hempstead, there were also straw, crock and cattle markets. The town itself tended to evolve around one street, the High Street.

The Market House and market buildings, which included the Women's Market House, selling dairy produce, were erected in the 17th century. A corn loft was built above it whilst a covered area underneath was available for market stalls. Nearby, the Butchers' Shambles had as many as 35 stalls, 15 being mentioned in the church terrier of 1708, and a further 20 are listed in the Bailiwick accounts. In the yards off the High Street were slaughterhouses, tanneries and blacksmiths, subsidiary trades for the requirements of the cattle markets.

THE MARKET HOUSE ZZZ03355 (Dacorum Heritage Trust Ltd)

This 18th-century print shows the Market House on the right with the sign of the King's Arms Inn to the left. The Swan Inn and the Cock Inn are just visible further down the street.

The Bailiwick made the regulations concerning the market and fairs and decided where the stalls should be placed in the High Street. According to the Bailiwick records, in 1629 the Bailiwick ruled that shoemakers should not stand in front of the King's Arms, and then in 1633 it was decreed that no stalls were to be erected on market days between the door of the Bell Inn and the door of the Cock, further down the street. As both the Bell and the King's Arms faced the Market House these decisions were probably taken to relieve congestion caused by carts, livestock and rubbish in the narrow street.

A constant check, by the Bailiwick, was kept on weights and measures together with early attempts to deal with food hygiene. The Bailiwick was therefore always concerned with the sale of unwholesome fish and attempted to supervise the slaughterhouses, which not only provided meat for the local trade but also for the London market. The Plait Market (see Chapter Three for the story of the plaiting industry), established at the beginning of the 19th century, was also to come under the supervision of the Bailiwick. According to Bailiwick records, in 1809 a penalty of £2 was imposed for the sale of plait before 8am between Michaelmas and Lady Day, and before 7am during the remainder of the year. This was to avoid the, 'great inconvenience and injury to the town' from the Plait Market.

The Manorial Court had considerable power in Hemel Hempstead, but it declined after the Reformation, when it became merely a recording agency for the sales and inheritance of land. The Bailiwick, however, gradually took on duties that would usually be dealt with by a Borough. Records show that it assumed responsibility for public health, lighting and a fire service. For example, in 1659 the Bailiwick paid Anthony Green of Lothbury, London, £30 for a fire engine. It also supervised highways, for in the Minute Book of 13 April 1725, it is recorded that 'as William Ivory had encroached his building on the street, the Bailiff and his Jury ordered it to be pulled down'. Although some of the powers were handed over to the Justices in the 18th century, the Bailiwick acted as the main agent for local government well into the 19th century.

HIGH STREET 1881 ZZZ03353 (Dacorum Heritage Trust Ltd)

The King's Arms is just beyond the boy standing in the foreground, with the Bell Inn further up the street.

People came from miles around as well as locally to attend the weekly market; consequently inns, alehouses and lodging houses sprang up on each side of the street. The inns were also used as meeting houses and places in which to conduct business transactions. At first innkeepers were mostly part-time landlords, and included people as diverse as a shoemaker, who was the landlord of the oldest inn, the Cock, in 1561, to William Fuller, landlord of the Bell in the 17th century, who was a surgeon. John Dickson, the landlord of the Rose and Crown in the early 18th century, managed to combine his trade as a plumber with that of landlord, an interesting combination.

Over the years some pubs disappeared altogether and others became private houses or other businesses. Many were squalid beerhouses that did not appear in trade directories. The larger inns are recorded in the Billeting Survey of 1756; for instance, Thomas Edge, the landlord of the Bell, owned the largest house in town, with nine beds and stabling for 54 horses. Apart from those in the High Street, more than 100 pubs and inns traded in Hemel Hempstead. The surfeit of pubs in the town was partly due to the Beer House Act of 1830-1869, which allowed anyone with a reasonable reputation to start a beer house upon a payment of two guineas to Customs and Excise.

After a decision of the Justices of Quarter Sessions for the need of a house of correction in Hemel Hempstead, this was established in 1664 at the north of the High Street, in a part of the Royal Oak's premises. With Christopher Mitchell appointed master, the house of correction was the first institution to be connected with the Poor Law, being a place where

vagrants and miscreants could be sent; by the end of the 17th century, however, the building was used as an ordinary jail. The inmates included deserters from the army or navy and men accused of fathering illegitimate children who might become a burden to the parish. It also provided accommodation for vagrants waiting to be returned to their home parishes by the authorities. Later the premises, which had remained a pub, became a common lodging house. The pub still traded until 1973.

Fact File

At one time there were 24 licensed premises in the High Street, now only four remain; the Bell, first registered as an inn in 1603; the King's Arms, established in 1626; the Rose and Crown, further down the street, built in 1523; and the White Hart, standing opposite, in 1605. Today, all four are brewery-managed houses and, in keeping with modern times, are theme pubs.

HIGH STREET c1890 ZZZ03358 (Dacorum Heritage Trust Ltd)

Next door to Lloyds Bank is the Boot, which closed in 1939, and three doors up and still trading is the Rose and Crown, with the White Hart opposite. The Half Moon, which closed in December 1912, is in the foreground to the left.

The expansion of the London Market was reflected in the enlarged and improved houses in the High Street. Many existing buildings were altered in the 1720s, for the leaden heads of rain pipes still bear initials and dates. Several houses had large gardens and orchards that were eventually built on, and infilling took place on open spaces between buildings. New buildings were also erected on such spare frontage land as remained and a continuous building line was established on each side of the street. In English towns, such as Hemel Hempstead, the period of rebuilding and improvement in the 18th century is known as the English Urban Renaissance.

HIGH STREET PRE 1888 ZZZ03359 (Dacorum Heritage Trust Ltd)

A woman stands outside the Royal Oak at the left of this 19th-century photograph.

recognised the strong Protestant and Nonconformist feeling in the town, together with the general support for Parliament.

A survey of the manor in the late 17th century contains few references to the High Street and this indicates that the copyhold land had been converted into freehold. This was a result of the Civil War when the Commonwealth Government sold Crown property to private individuals. Following the restoration of Charles II in 1660, the Manor of Hemel Hempstead was returned to the Crown. In 1702, the manor was leased to the Halsey family, who purchased it in 1815.

THE OLD BELL, HIGH STREET 2005 H255707k
(Peter Grainger)

The Georgian front was simply tacked onto the old, with the original inn becoming a house within a house.

Further royal charters were also granted to Hemel Hempstead, but these mainly related to matters concerning the manor. However, the Charter of the Lord Protector Cromwell, granted 26 February 1656, was to be of importance to the development of the town. This charter gave to the inhabitants of Hemel Hempstead three extra annual fairs, so that they might receive 'all lawful profits of the three said fairs'. Although Oliver Cromwell had allowed a measure of religious tolerance, he nevertheless

St Mary's Church supplies us with evidence of the reception given by the townspeople to the proclamation of, and coronation of, William and Mary in 1689. When the weathervane was taken down for repairs after bad weather in 1927, Robert Gregory, Bailiff 1690, and the names of two churchwardens were found inscribed on it. The weathervane may have been erected by public subscription as a mark of Protestant sympathy. Bailiwick records show that Dutch soldiers were entertained in the town, and large quantities of wine and beer were consumed. During the hectic celebrations the Bailiff's staff was broken and repaired at a cost of 6d (2.5p). It can still be seen in the Civic Centre.

HEMEL HEMPSTEAD c1955 H255017

The Manor of Hemel Hempstead remained in the ownership of the Halsey family until it was acquired by the Hemel Hempstead Development Corporation in 1946 in order to build the New Town.

After the setback of a fire in the market buildings in 1749, the High Street recovered with the establishment of new trades and businesses. More specialised shops began to appear such as barbers, grocers, drapers and hatters. However, as the town grew it could not extend westwards, to what is now Gadebridge Park, because this land was owned by the Combe family, and later became the estate of Sir Astley Paston Cooper. To the south was a road, now known as Marlowes, that was a continuation of the High Street, but this was a boggy area and was slow to be developed. Consequently, when Hemel Hempstead expanded it did so in a very unusual fashion, spreading through the alleys and inn yards on the east side of the High Street, into strip-like developments. Here cottages were erected and outbuildings

and cellars were converted into dwellings that quickly became slums.

During the 18th century, the roads Cherry Bounce, Chapel Street, Bell Road (now St Mary's Road), and George Street were all developing on the east side of the of the High Street and were in effect extensions of the main street. At the southern end of the High Street the road branched to the east into Saffron Lane, later known as Queen Street. At one time the High Street stretched to the west, to the south of Gadebridge Park, when the land there formed the grounds of the Bury. This short stretch of road, which joined Bury Road to the west with Queen Street, now Lower Queensway, became known as Broadway. It obtained the name because it was a 'broad way' when compared to the narrow High Street. With the wide expanse at the top of Marlowes, this area became an overflow for the cattle market. By the end of the 18th century, however, the cattle market was dismantled and the London entrance to the town, as it was known, was improved. The cattle market was moved to a meadow behind the Rose and Crown. As the last specialised market of Hemel Hempstead, it survived up to the Second World War. Marlowes itself was gradually developed with several fine villas and shops appearing amongst speculative building and shabby cottages.

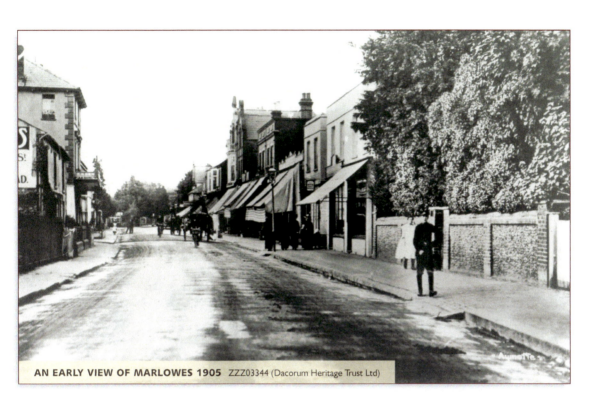

AN EARLY VIEW OF MARLOWES 1905   ZZZ03344 (Dacorum Heritage Trust Ltd)

MARLOWES c1965   H255007

The charters of Henry VIII allowed a fair to be held at the feast of Corpus Christi. The Statute or 'Statty Fair' was a hiring fair for farm servants that took place on 3 September under the control of the Bailiff. Men and women who wished to be hired stood in line at the top of the High Street dressed in their smocks and carrying the emblems of their trade. Gradually, through falling receipts, the Bailiff's supervision ceased and the fair, in a very different form, moved to the Rose and Crown meadow, and was run by professional showmen. The Meadow was eventually built on, and is now known as Fig Tree Hill. New flats and houses were erected there in the late 1950s.

Closely connected with the Bailiwick was the Box Moor Trust, which to this day is still responsible for some 400 acres of land to the south-west of the old town. Box Moor consists of moorland, commons, and various meadows. On 19 July 1574 Elizabeth I gave the moor, which was part of the Manor of Hemel Hempstead, to Robert, Earl of Leicester. He sold the property the next day to the Earl of Bedford and Peter Graye of Leicester. In 1581 it was acquired by three local inhabitants, John Rolfe, William Gladman, and Richard Pope for the sum of £75. They probably raised the money by public subscription because a later deed conveyed the moor to 67 inhabitants of Hemel Hempstead and Bovingdon, a village three miles from the moor. The deed was witnessed by Francis Combe of The Bury and Richard Gawton, the Vicar of St Mary's.

The moor was administered by twelve feoffees (trustees). In 1809 a private Act of Parliament effectively vested the trust's assets in these twelve trustees. The properties owned by the trust included 29 dwelling houses, workshops, barns and, at one time, five pubs. How the rents and profits from the Box Moor Trust were used was supposedly a decision by a majority of the householders at meetings in the Vestry rooms at Hemel Hempstead and Bovingdon. However, as the same citizens were usually elected to serve as Trustees of Box Moor, members of the Bailiwick Jury and the Vestry, all at the same time, there appears to have been no problem, especially in the 19th century, deciding how the money should be spent.

BOX MOOR 2005 H255708k (Peter Grainger)

THE CANAL, BOXMOOR 2005 H255709k (Peter Grainger)

In 1797 a committee of seven was appointed by the trustees to negotiate with the proprietors of the newly formed Grand Junction Canal Company who required land for the extension of their canal. Some 25 acres were sold for £900. The canal flowed past the south of Hemel Hempstead, across the moor where it followed the London Road.

HEATH PARK c1955 H255011

The canal meets the River Gade at Heath Park, to the south of Marlowes. Two portions of the moor were leased to Hemel Hempstead Borough Council who provided a recreational area and a bandstand in the 1920s. There was also a children's playground near to where the Kodak building now stands. These all disappeared when the New Town was being developed in the 1950s.

The sale of the land to the canal company enabled the trust to build Boxmoor Wharf and a workhouse. The wharf then became the main coal wharf serving the town. In the late 1890s, Henry Balderson, who was Mayor of the Borough of Hemel Hempstead in 1900, used the wharf to import wines and spirits. The wharf was later leased to Rose's who shipped raw lime juice from London direct to the wharf by means of the canal. Since 1986 Boxmoor Wharf has been leased to B & Q Stores. (The village and surrounding districts are known as Boxmoor, but the moor itself is referred to as Box Moor).

HEATH PARK c1955 H255010

The council acquired Churchill House and grounds in 1934, and built an open-air swimming pool. The modern sports centre now stands on the site (hidden by the trees).

BOXMOOR WHARF c1920 ZZZ03347 (Dacorum Heritage Trust Ltd)

AN INVOICE OF HENRY BALDERSON 1885 ZZZ04373
(Reproduced by courtesy of Dacorum Borough Council Archives)

Constant fear of highway robbery was a great concern for travellers, but the highwayman Robert Snooks caught the popular imagination, and to this day he is a regarded as a local 'hero'. In 1801, John Stevens, a post boy, was making his round to Hemel Hempstead from Tring, when he was held up and robbed by Snooks at Boxmoor. Later Snooks was caught, and at his trial at Hertford he was sentenced to be hanged on the Moor on 11 March 1802.

Fact File

When Snooks was being brought from Hertford to Boxmoor, the coach stopped at a local pub, the Bird in Hand, for Snooks to have a final drink. Snooks apparently called out to the crowds rushing to see the execution that 'It's no good hurrying they can't start the fun until I get there.'

SNOOKS'S GRAVE ZZZ03354 (Dacorum Heritage Trust Ltd)

The execution was supervised by John Page, the High Constable. It appears that the horse was whipped up, the cart was drawn away from beneath the gallows tree and Snooks was left hanging. The body was placed in a shallow grave, but the next day local inhabitants paid for a coffin. The Box Moor Trustees later provided a headstone, which initially had to be placed at the foot of the grave, this being the correct procedure for the burial of a highwayman. It was later placed at the head of the grave and can still be seen on Box Moor (on the moor opposite Hemel Hempstead station, past the railway bridge). Robert Snooks was the last highwayman to be hanged at the scene of his crime.

The main London Road followed the course of the River Bulbourne across the moor. The canal of 1797 and the railway, which arrived in 1837, also followed the same route. The 19th century was not only a century of industrialisation but also one of Free Trade and to be bypassed by these important means of communication was to have serious consequences for the town. However, the increase in the population at Boxmoor was attributed in the 1871 census, as being due to 'the proximity of rail and canal.'

In 1840 an open-air swimming pool was constructed on Box Moor, opposite to where St John's Church now stands. Known as the Boxmoor Baths, the pool was filled with unheated and untreated water from the canal and even included newts and fish. However, the Baths remained popular with the local people until the provision of new Churchill swimming pool of the 1930s.

The Box Moor Trustees were required to regulate the number of cattle and horses on the moor. So in 1809, each house in Hemel Hempstead and Bovingdon, with grazing rights, was assigned a ticket. The number of tickets required varied for different animals, and the grazier was at liberty to buy unwanted tickets. Later, Joseph Cranstone, who was elected a trustee on 29 May 1833, was instructed on 14 September of the same year, to make 800 plaques in his High Street iron foundry. These plaques were then fixed to every house in the area entitled to grazing rights on the moor. This was the first of several orders for Cranstone from the trust, and others such as fencing and gates followed swiftly. The Bulbourne Bridge was also constructed by Cranstone at the cost of £84.0.3d. On Tuesday 22 December 1846, during a special meeting of the trustees, Joseph Cranstone was elected permanent chairman of the trust, a position he held until his death in 1878.

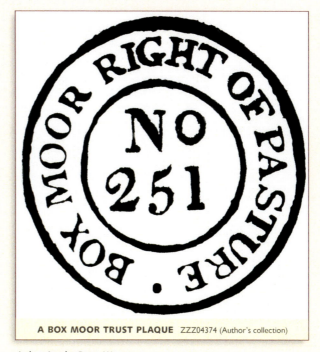

A BOX MOOR TRUST PLAQUE ZZZ04374 (Author's collection)

A drawing by Peter Wagon.

BOXMOOR WHARF c1920 ZZZ03347 (Dacorum Heritage Trust Ltd)

ST JOHN'S ROAD, BOXMOOR 1906 ZZZ03357 (Dacorum Heritage Trust Ltd)

Over the years Boxmoor village has hardly changed. The Roman Catholic Church, St Mary and St Joseph, was built in St John's Road in 1898. The present Victorian Gothic Church of St John the Evangelist, built in April 1874 on the moor, replaced the 1829 Chapel of Ease.

To this day, the Moor provides excellent recreational facilities. The Hemel Hempstead Cricket Club plays at Heath Park, and Boxmoor Cricket Club plays on the 'Oval' in St John's Road. Hemel Hempstead (Camelot) Rugby Club use Chaulden Meadow.

Even though Boxmoor village has survived, it was destined to be surrounded by the New Town. Northridge Way, to the west of the village, was one of the new roads that led to the neighbourhoods of Chaulden and Warners End.

LONG CHAULDEN c1965 H255084

Long Chaulden, part of the New Town, leads to Chaulden Meadow.

BOXTED ROAD, WARNERS END c1965 H255099

ORDNANCE SURVEY MAP SHOWING HEMEL HEMPSTEAD 1897

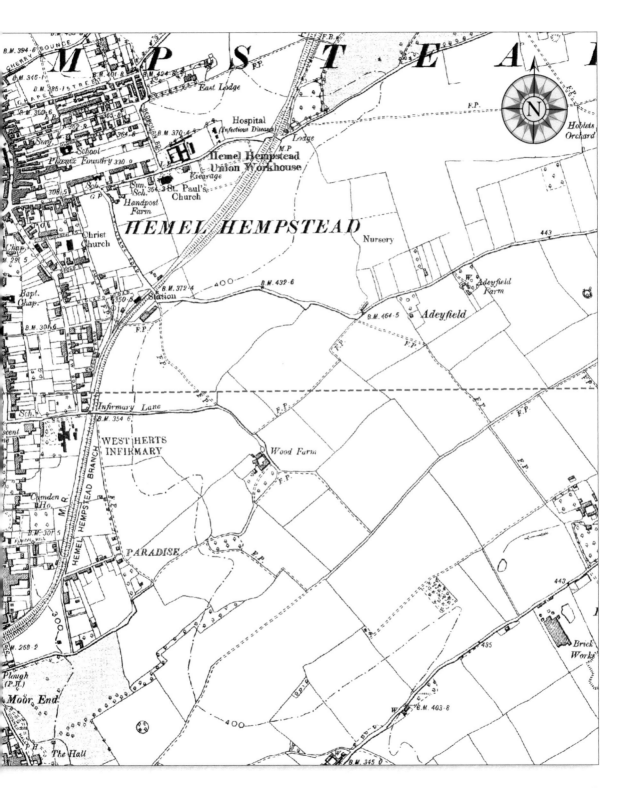

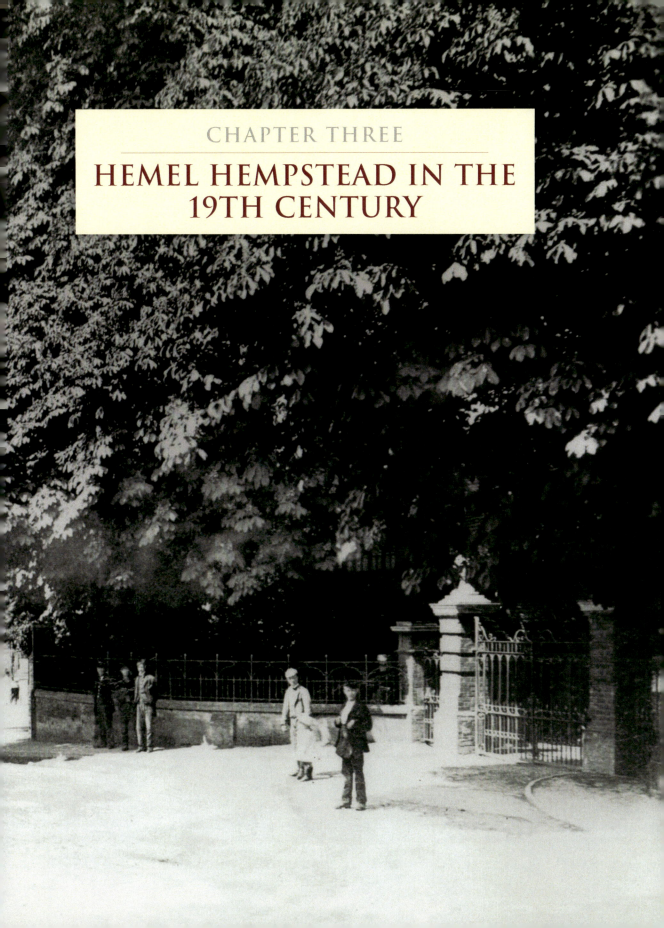

CHAPTER THREE

HEMEL HEMPSTEAD IN THE 19TH CENTURY

UNTIL JOHN DICKINSON established his paper mills at Apsley at the beginning of the 19th century, there was no specialised industrial development in the town. As with most market towns of the time, industries, such as tanneries and breweries, mainly existed in Hemel Hempstead to provide for local needs. The majority of the population was employed in agriculture but, as the 19th century progressed, the once rural town gradually changed.

Before the beginning of the 19th century paper had been made by hand. Nicholas Louis Robert, a Frenchman, invented a way of making paper in a continuous web in 1798. Two London stationers, Henry and Sealy Fourdrinier, bought the patents, and in 1803 they were producing paper at Frogmore Mill, an old corn mill, at Apsley. However, by

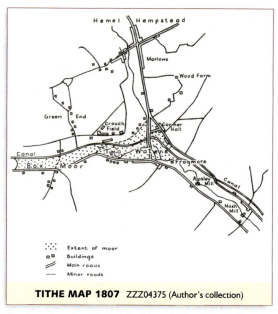

TITHE MAP 1807 ZZZ04375 (Author's collection)

Produced and published by Hemel Hempstead History Society, 1972.

1810 the Fourdriniers were bankrupt due to the expense of developing the new process. Henry Fourdrinier did not renew his lease of Frogmore Mill in 1816, and in 1817 it was bought by the Grand Junction Canal Company. In spite of his financial difficulties, Henry Fourdrinier was elected Bailiff of Hemel Hempstead in 1815.

John Dickinson, (1782-1869), the founder of John Dickinson & Co Ltd, set up in business in 1804 when he went into partnership with George Longman of the book publishing family in London. Meanwhile, Dickinson had invented what became known as the cylinder mould machine and after he had patented his invention in 1809, he decided to exploit it. As papermaking requires water, it was the canal that first encouraged John Dickinson to buy Apsley Mill. Two years

APSLEY MILLS c1920 ZZZ03348
(Dacorum Heritage Trust Ltd)

This photograph was taken before extensions to the mills, which replaced Apsley Vicarage and Salmon Meadow, were built. When the mills eventually closed, a Sainsbury's supermarket was built on part of the site and opened on 5 May 1993, by the Mayor of Dacorum, John Buteux.

later, in 1811, Dickinson bought Nash Mills, where the canal runs between London Road and Belswains Lane, and both mills were converted to papermaking.

There was a long dispute between the Grand Union Canal and John Dickinson, who claimed that water was lost from the Gade into the canal to the detriment of the two mills. A settlement with the Canal Company, by an Act of Parliament in 1818, enabled the canal to be diverted along the course of the Gade close by Apsley and Nash Mills. The canal linked Apsley Mill, Nash Mills and, as the firm expanded, the mills at Home Park and Croxley. The horse-drawn barges would transport coal, raw materials and rags to the mills, whilst the finished paper products would be loaded at the south bay at Apsley Mills for the return journey to Paddington for worldwide distribution.

By 1824 both mills were being operated by steam power, giving employment to the local population. At Apsley Mills, for example, over 60 men and a large number of women and children were employed. By 1881, the total number employed at the mill was 471, including 256 women and girls. The Education Acts of 1870 and 1880 meant that children were no longer employed.

SAINSBURY'S, APSLEY MILLS 2005 H255710k (Peter Grainger)

APSLEY LOCK 2005 H255711k (Peter Grainger)

JOHN DICKINSON WORKERS c1900 ZZZ03345 (Dacorum Heritage Trust Ltd)

John Dickinson patented over 20 inventions and was to revolutionise the paper making industry. This led to the production of an ever increasing number of paper products, and some of the trade names which were developed, such as Basildon Bond writing paper, became known through the worldwide market. By the 20th century Dickinson's paper mills were to become amongst the largest in the world. It was the success of the mills that led to the development of Apsley.

Harry Grover was the leading solicitor in Hemel Hempstead and, with his partner James Pollard, he owned the first bank in Hemel Hempstead, located at what is now 27 High Street. Country banks played an important role during the Industrial Revolution, and Dickinson's mills were only possible thanks to the support of the Grover-Pollard Bank. In 1810 John Dickinson married Harry Grover's second child, Ann. Gradually, Dickinson came to be accepted into Hertfordshire society. He subscribed towards the building of a church at Leverstock Green, and in 1847 he built a little school at Nash Mills at his own expense. He gave the land, by Kings Langley railway station, for the building of the Booksellers Provident Retreat. Its opening on 3 September 1845 may be said to mark his acceptance as a local landowner.

John Dickinson invested in 125 acres to the east of Nash Mills, and built himself a fine house that he called Abbots Hill. He was his own architect, with a theory that no house should have more than one door to the outside world. His wife, Ann, disagreed, as she wrote that 'the odious house' was built against her wishes.

NASH MILLS ZZZ03346 (Dacorum Heritage Trust Ltd)

John Dickinson's house, Abbots Hill, is shown on the hill to the left, in Abbots Langley. The mills are in Hemel Hempstead, and the canal lock to the right of the mills is No 68.

In 1800 the population of the parish was 3,680, and at this time of Hemel Hempstead was practically confined to the old town. In contrast to the development of industry at Apsley, straw plaiting, a cottage industry, flourished in the town of Hemel Hempstead, the villages of Boxmoor, Leverstock Green and Piccotts End. It gave employment, however poorly paid, to many local women and children.

The straw plaiting industry, which became a significant feature of local commerce in the 19th century, was closely connected with agriculture in Hertfordshire. When the French Wars stopped imports of foreign plait, the hat manufacturers of Luton, Dunstable and St Albans became dependent on local home plaiters.

Sometimes the plaiters bought their straw from a local farmer but most bought their straw from a plait dealer. He would be a middleman bringing the straw from the farmer and selling it to the plaiters. Living in the High Street, Mary Grout, for example, was a straw sorter who worked for her father. He was a straw dealer and one of the middlemen who supplied the plaiters with straw. The Grouts also had a straw factory and employed several children living near by.

Women and children plaited straw to supplement the meagre family income. Even when the price of plait fell in the middle of the 19th century, a woman aided by her children could add 12 shillings (60p) a week to the family income, more than the agricultural wage of 9-10 shillings (45-50p).

Fact File

The middlemen often had a bad reputation as this rhyme reveals, warning the young girls employed in the trade -

'In Buckingham and Hertfordshire
Mind maiden what you're at.
And shun the naughty married men
Who deal in ladies plait'

Apart from the better-off traders and shopkeepers, nearly every family had members who plaited. Perhaps the saddest story is of a girl named Martha Irons. She plaited for long hours during the 1850s in order to pay for her keep at the Brewers Arms, a beer and lodging house, for it appears that Martha was an orphan and only eight years old.

The 1851 census is misleading as most of the children listed as 'scholars' attended plait schools, which were not educational establishments. Most of the schoolteachers in the census for Hemel Hempstead were located in Marlowes running private day and boarding academies. So it could be assumed that the children of the growing middle class, listed as scholars, attended these schools. On the other hand, the only other school in the High Street was the plait school run by Elizabeth Watts, near the old tithe barn off Half Moon Yard. It is not difficult to see which school would have been favoured by the labouring poor for their children.

At plait schools the parents provided the straw and paid a fee of about three pence a week. It was rare for any other subject to be taught as most of the keepers of plait schools were illiterate and some, such as Elizabeth Watts, were both illiterate and unable to plait. The yardstick by which parents judged a teacher's ability was the success with which she wielded her osier stick to make the children work.

The misery of the long hours and the strict discipline in the plait schools is revealed in the Children's Employment Commission of 1864, where the overcrowded schools appear to have been places of exceptional squalor. Boys as well as girls started plaiting at the age of four or even earlier, as in the case of Mary Ann Britt, aged three, who lived in the High Street.

The children were taught to plait with both hands whilst moistening the next straws in their mouth. Consequently many children developed unsightly cracks at the corner of their mouths. A supply of straw was held under the left arm leaving some children with a hunched left shoulder. Whilst lack of exercise led to stunted growth, catarrhal infections, sore mouths and crooked fingers were also occupational hazards. After the Education Acts of 1870 and 1880, making elementary education compulsory, truancy was high in the board and village schools. At George Street School, for example, parents kept their children away in order to plait straw. As a result, this area was educationally one of the most backward in the county.

KING'S ARMS YARD 2005 H255712k (Peter Grainger)

Held in Collet's Yard, on the east side of the High Street, the Plait Market was moved to King's Arms Yard in 1832.

What life was like for the unfortunate plait children can be gleaned from a Factory Inspector's report in 1870. He associated their mothers, the plait women, with 'vacant minds, dirty cottages and neglected children'. The decline of the plait schools was caused mainly by the deterioration of the plait industry; aided by the fact that from 1891 education was not only compulsory, it was also free. The 19th century was a century of Free Trade and this allowed cheap plait imports from Italy and later from China and Japan. Plaits that were sold for one shilling (10p) a score in 1838, were only fetching 3d (1.5p) in 1893. By the 1870s an experienced plaiter's earnings had dropped to about four shillings a week.

In spite of the hardships, straw plaiting provided a much-needed income for the labouring poor and opportunities for the aged and widows, who otherwise would become a burden on the parish. The craft, the way of life of the plaiters, together with their independent spirit, has endured in local memory.

At the other end of the social scale, the arrival in the early 19th century of the gentry in the form of the Cooper family provided a noticeable Tory-Anglican form of interference into local affairs. The people of Hemel Hempstead, who during the Middle Ages were ruled by the rector and monks at Ashridge, now found themselves under the stewardship of the gentry who lived at Gadebridge. Indeed, the Cooper family interfered with life in Hemel Hempstead in a way that the Lords of the Manor, the Halsey family, never did.

GADEBRIDGE HOUSE 1952 ZZZ03340 (Dacorum Heritage Trust Ltd)

Gadebridge House and estate was purchased for the town by the Hemel Hempstead Borough Council in 1952. The house became a preparatory school for boys until 1963 and was demolished when Kodak bought the site. When Kodak moved the site was developed for housing.

Sir Astley Paston Cooper (1768-1841) was the most distinguished British surgeon of his day. In 1800 he was appointed Surgeon to Guy's Hospital and was elected a Fellow of the Royal Society in 1802. His private practice became the largest that any surgeon had ever had and among his many famous and rich patients were King George IV, the Duke of Wellington and Sir Robert Peel. In 1821, after the successful removal of a tumour on the king's head, Professor Cooper was created a Baronet.

Sir Astley spent much time at his Gadebridge estate, which is now Gadebridge Park. He married Ann Cocks on 12 December 1791, but their only child Anne Maria and their adopted daughter Sarah both died young. Without an heir, Sir Astley was succeeded on his death in 1841 by his nephew, Astley Paston Cooper, who became the 2nd Baronet. He married Elizabeth Rickford, the only child and heiress of William Rickford, MP for Aylesbury. They had ten sons and three daughters, the eldest son succeeding his father as the 3rd Baronet on 6 January 1866.

Until the end of the 19th century local landowners as Justices of the Peace were all powerful. Thus Sir Astley, the 1st Baronet, was a magistrate for Hertfordshire and his great nephew, the 3rd Baronet, was a magistrate for both Hertfordshire and Suffolk, and also became High Sheriff of Hertfordshire in 1885. They were all elected to the Jury and the 1st Baronet was elected Bailiff in 1825. The 3rd Baronet held office in 1873 and his youngest brother, Clement Astley Paston Cooper, who was also a JP, became Bailiff

Amongst landowners there was often a paternalistic belief that it was their duty to help the poor and many, including Sir Astley Paston Cooper, the 1st Baronet, made substantial contributions to society. He founded the infirmary at Piccotts End, which opened for 'the gracious relief of the necessitous poor' in January 1827. It was transferred in 1831 to the West Herts Infirmary, at Marlowes, Hemel Hempstead, endowed and built by another landowner, Sir John Saunders Sebright. Throughout the rest of the century the Sebrights were the greatest benefactors to the hospital.

in 1885. The 3rd Baronet became the first mayor on 9 November 1898. Although the 2nd Baronet did not hold office, he interfered in the Bailiwick's affairs, whether it be the construction of the gas works or the building of the new Town Hall. Instead of the Bailiff, he presided over all the Bailiwick functions, including the prestigious Wool Fair Dinner.

Just how far the gentry could use their political influence is illustrated by the coming of the railway. Robert Stephenson's original plan for the construction of the London and Birmingham Railway was to take the line through the Dagnall Gap and Hemel Hempstead. As the route was planned to pass through the Gade Valley it included the land belonging to Sir Astley Paston Cooper, at Gadebridge, which flanked the west of the High Street. When Sir Astley forced a re-routing this could only spell disaster for the traders in the High Street, as it was later proposed to by-pass the town with a route following the main London Road and canal at Box Moor. The citizens' petitions and protests to the railway company were simply ignored. Later in the century, with the town cut off from the main forms of transport, the Bailiwick supported a scheme in 1887 for a steam tramway to connect Chesham to Boxmoor, Apsley and the High Street at Alexandra Road. The plan never materialised due to strong opposition from Sir Astley, the 3rd Baronet.

In Hemel Hempstead, the Religious Census of 1851 revealed the ascendancy of the Nonconformists and the successful innkeepers and traders now demanded status to accompany their economic achievements. The struggle in the middle classes was for control of the Bailiwick, where the office of Bailiff was the highest position a local citizen could hold.

THE VIEW ALONG BROADWAY, LOOKING WEST 1881 ZZZ03343 (Dacorum Heritage Trust Ltd)

A posting house was built opposite the entrance to Gadebridge, and stood on the site now occupied by West Herts College. A horse-drawn bus owned by the LNWR (London & North Western Railway) linked the High Street with the station at Boxmoor. The drinking fountain, built by Joseph Cranstone in 1835, now stands outside Boxmoor Hall.

Few people living in Hemel Hempstead appear to have been so committed to local politics as the Quaker, Joseph Cranstone (1794-1878). He entered the political arena in 1838, when as a Reformer he lost the contested election for the office of Bailiff. Yet Joseph's greatest achievement was his election as Bailiff the following year, 1839/1840, when he presided over the public celebrations at the marriage of Queen Victoria. He thus obtained a political office commensurate with his business success. William Henry, Joseph's fourteenth child, took over the family business when Joseph retired in 1867, and was elected Bailiff in 1871/1872. After their terms of office, both remained on the Jury, Joseph until 1878 and William Henry until 1898. Joseph was elected to the Board of Guardians from 1865 to 1874. He was also a member of all the important Committees such as the Town Hall Committee and the prestigious Wool Fair Committee.

J. HALES,

High Art

DECORATOR,

AND

SANITARY

PLUMBER, &c.

....

26, MARLOWES,

HEMEL HEMPSTEAD

ADVERTISEMENT FOR JOSIAH HALES ZZZ04376
(Reproduced by courtesy of Dacorum Borough Council Archives)

Josiah Hales, a wealthy plumber and decorator, was Bailiff in 1849. Like Joseph Cranstone, Josiah also had a finger in every pie. After his first wife died, Josiah married Joseph Cranstone's fifth child, Eliza, on 10 October 1854.

In small towns such as Hemel Hempstead, gas lighting caught the imagination of both the Bailiwick and the townspeople, whilst the pressing problems of drains and clean water supply attracted little interest. On 27 March 1835 the Bailiwick resolved to form a company called the Hemel Hempstead Gas, Light and Coke Company for the purpose of lighting the town. Among the trustees of the new company was Sir Astley Paston Cooper, with Joseph Cranstone and the Bailiff, Charles Grover, as directors. After registration of the company, the eight board members selected a piece of land at Bury Road where Joseph Cranstone built the gas works. On 1 September 1835 the Bailiwick recorded that the town was lit by gas for the first time when 'many hundreds of spectators came from all parts to witness the event'. The Bailiwick bought 20 lamps in total, paying 50 shillings (£2.50) per lamp to the Gas Company, who also supplied the iron posts and lamps. These were made by Joseph Cranstone's iron foundry.

To celebrate the use of gas for street lighting, the Bailiff, together with 40 gentlemen, including Sir Astley Paston Cooper and Joseph Cranstone, and the directors of the Gas Company, attended a dinner cooked by gas at the Market House. The Bailiwick records state that 'many hundreds of persons were admitted to witness the process of cooking by gas'.

On 4 February 1851 Sir Astley Paston Cooper, Joseph Cranstone and Josiah Hales were appointed to serve on a committee for the building of a new Town Hall. In spite of the presence of Sir Astley Paston Cooper, the 2nd Baronet, the new Town Hall was a symbol of the ascendancy of the middle classes in local government. According to the Bailiwick records, the site of the old Market House, which was to be demolished, was considered 'sufficient for the purpose' of

THE TOWN HALL 1852 ZZZ03342
(Dacorum Heritage Trust Ltd)

building the new Town Hall. Designed by the architect George Lowe and built by the firm of William Sears, the Gothic-style building was completed by 1852. The building was not as large as it is today and consisted of the section north of the present main entrance. The section up to St Mary's Close was to be added later.

Civic pride had to be paid for in hard cash, so a subscription list was published on 28 June 1853. Unfortunately the cost of the Town Hall was more than anticipated by the Bailiwick, so the Box Moor Trust came to the aid of the Bailiwick and contributed £1,278. The Town Hall was originally built over an open colonnade, looking as it does today, but it was enclosed in 1857 to make a corn exchange, thus incurring more expense. On Saturday, 30 March 1861 the county newspaper, The Hertford Mercury, reported that the Bailiwick proposed to extend the Town Hall by adding a reading room with a Vestry room below, the cost of £463 being met by a loan from the Bucks and Oxon Bank. In 1868 the Bailiwick took out another loan to pay for a new corn loft, whilst continuing to rely on the Box Moor Trust to clear the building debt.

The gates at the entrance to the Town Hall were erected to mark William Henry Cranstone's term in office as Bailiff, 1871/1872. The names on the subscription list for the gates show that all the members of the local gentry, including the Coopers, contributed.

According to the Bailiwick Records dated 31 December 1886, 'The Corporation purchased the Lamb Inn, to pull down for

THE BUTCHERS' SHAMBLES AND LAMB INN 1881 ZZZ03351 (Dacorum Heritage Trust Ltd)

public improvements'. The Butchers' Shambles was also demolished. A market place and Civic buildings with shops were built on the site of the Lamb Inn. This was rather grandly named the New Promenade.

As a result of these extensions a debt of £1,500 was owed to the Bank. Times, however, were changing and the Box Moor Trust decided that it would no longer subsidise the Bailiwick. In addition, in 1898 the trust built Boxmoor Hall, which became a rival to the Town Hall with respect to lettings.

Several posters advertising the events that took place in the Town Hall provide us with a great deal of information about how people lived. One poster advertises an auction of china together with cut glass items and earthenware goods to be held in the autumn of 1870. The Industrial Revolution meant that mass-produced goods reached even humble homes, and the poorer people of Hemel Hempstead would certainly have bought earthenware goods, especially teapots. They would also attend second-hand clothing auctions, which were also advertised. Property auctions would have interested the wealthier members of the town.

THE VIEW PAST THE TOWN HALL, LOOKING SOUTH c1890 ZZZ03350 (Dacorum Heritage Trust Ltd)

The main hall, situated on the first floor of the Town Hall, was used by the Justices of the Peace for Petty Sessions and was a venue of the town's social events. It was used as a meeting place for a Natural History Society, philosophic discussions, dinners and balls. Posters reveal that cheap seats were available at the music halls, so the poorer classes could also enjoy them.

Apart from the Wool Fair Dinner, the most prestigious event was the Bailiff's Dinner. Invitations, table plans and menus that have survived indicate that the banquet was an all-male occasion. Enormous amounts of food were consumed, and there were always at least 17 toasts to be proposed and replied to. The caterers frequently claimed for damages from the Bailiwick. For example, Mary Jones, the proprietress of the Bell, claimed £1.2s 0d (£1.10) for broken glasses after Mr Roberts, the solicitor and auctioneer, celebrated his election as Bailiff in 1850. By 1880, however, the ladies were also invited to the Bailiff's Dinner, which consequently became a far more sedate affair.

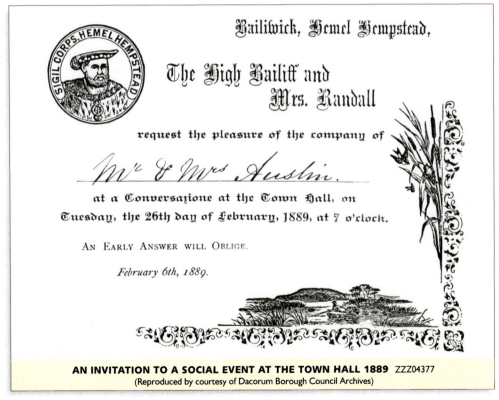

AN INVITATION TO A SOCIAL EVENT AT THE TOWN HALL 1889 ZZZ04377
(Reproduced by courtesy of Dacorum Borough Council Archives)

The Town Hall is not only the largest building in the High Street, it is also sited at the focal point of the area and reflected the Bailiwick's civic pride. The building as a whole represents a notable monument to the high-Victorian period.

THE BUTCHERS' SHAMBLES AND LAMB INN 1881 ZZZ03351 (Dacorum Heritage Trust Ltd)

HIGH STREET 1881 ZZZ03352 (Dacorum Heritage Trust Ltd)

At right foreground is Joseph Cranstone's 1848 pump. Cranstone also installed another water pump at the shambles, in 1836. In the background, known locally as the Dip, are the former beer houses: the Old King's Head, the Brewer's Arms and the Coach and Horses. Opposite, is the now closed Sun Inn.

Apart from John Dickinson with his successful mills at Apsley, no one contributed more to the town's development than Joseph Cranstone, aided later by his son, William Henry. In 1857 Joseph purchased the Cock Inn at 23 High Street, which stood next door to his ironmonger's shop, in order to extend his engineering works. Eventually it became known as the Phoenix Works and exhibited at many of the important trade fairs in the country.

In the mid-Victorian period Hemel Hempstead was the centre of a large agricultural district and a steady part of the Cranstone business had to do with serving the needs of this community. Agriculture was chiefly arable, for which the greatest variety of machinery was available. Thus, the Cranstones advertised in Pigot's Directory of 1867 that they sold and repaired agricultural machinery of every description.

Fact File

Joseph Cranstone built an early steam-driven road motor and made the journey from Hemel Hempstead to London. However, on the return journey the vehicle ran backwards and crashed on Stanmore Hill. Joseph was unhurt apart from his pride it seems, for no public records or newspaper reports remain of the incident.

A WILLIAM HENRY CRANSTONE BILL HEAD 1875
ZZZ04378 (Reproduced by courtesy of
Dacorum Borough Council Archives)

HEMEL HEMPSTEAD FIRE BRIGADE 1905 ZZZ03341 (Dacorum Heritage Trust Ltd)

Joseph Cranstone formed the Volunteer Fire Brigade in 1845 and acted as its superintendent for 33 years. Other brigade members included Josiah Hales, and his son from his first marriage, and eleven other volunteers. There were also twelve paid men. Later, William Henry took over from his father. A fire engine house stood at the entrance to Gadebridge, and a new Fire Station was built on the site in 1905. The building, part of a pseudo-Tudor block, still stands in Queensway.

Joseph Cranstone's iron works produced two fire engines, one for the Volunteer Fire Brigade and the other for the Phoenix Assurance Company. The Phoenix fire engine was owned by the town's Phoenix Fire-Office and maintained, as agents, by Joseph and later

A PHOENIX FIRE-OFFICE RECEIPT 1881 ZZZ04379
(Reproduced by courtesy of Dacorum Borough Council Archives)

William Henry, to protect property insured with the Phoenix. Accounts show that the Bailiwick contributed to the other engine, and Josiah Hales was paid £6 per year for 'attendance on parish fire engine'.

The secret of the Cranstones' success appears to be the control of local politics,

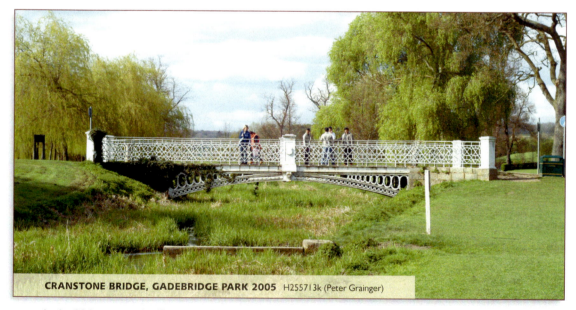

CRANSTONE BRIDGE, GADEBRIDGE PARK 2005 H255713k (Peter Grainger)

In the 20th century, the Cranstone Phoenix Works merged with the Hemel Hempstead Engineering Company led by the Christopher family. In 1949, with the planning of the New Town, the Foundry moved to Cupid Green and was demolished in 1984.

which enabled them to claim the patronage of various organisations such as the Box Moor Trust and the Bailiwick. The political alliance between the Reformer Joseph Cranstone and the Tory Coopers with regard to the building of the Town Hall and the setting up of the Hemel Hempstead Gas Light and Coke Company stood the Cranstones in good stead. All orders for gas fittings and gas stoves for the new Town Hall went to the Cranstone Company. The Cooper family were also valued customers, for the wrought iron bridge over the River Gade, which gave access to their home, has the name 'Cranstone' on it.

The Public Health Inquiry of 1854 revealed a high death rate in the town due to unsanitary conditions and the pollution of the water supply. In spite of 94 ratepayers petitioning for the implementation of the Public Health Act of 1848 and actions by the Board of Guardians, which constantly referred to 'defects in the sanitary state of their districts', few improvements were made.

According to the report of the 1854 inquiry, the sewerage of the town was confined to the High Street area. Cherry Bounce was the first to be condemned as a slum area. The main sewer in the High Street was only deep enough to carry off rain and surface water with an out-fall into an open ditch; in times of heavy rain the whole High Street was flooded. The courts and yards occupied by the 'labouring people' had little or no drainage and these areas were covered with 'the filthiest garbage'. To make matters worse, the yards were also occupied by pigs, slaughter-houses, stabling and dunghills.

The absence of any town planning in the expanding towns in the 19th century created problems not only in accommodation but also for the health of inhabitants, due to poor sanitation. Whilst the middle classes of Hemel Hempstead enjoyed a comfortable lifestyle, conditions were very different in the more densely populated areas in the town. The poor crowded into houses which were divided and subdivided, with outbuildings and cellars also occupied. Many cottages were owned by local tradesmen, usually built for speculative purposes. In 1848, James Cross, for example, built his butcher's shop on the corner of Cherry Bounce. Further up the lane he constructed a row of two-roomed dwellings that were an invitation to become slums.

Hemel Hempstead had a high mortality rate with 30 people dying of fever in 1851. Mr Robert Merry, the Surgeon and Medical Officer of the Workhouse Union, claimed that in most of the fever cases, the cause could be traced to some filthy open ditch or stagnant pool in the neighbourhood. It was plain therefore, the report concluded, that the town was deteriorating rather than progressing. It was not until 1896 that the much-needed sewerage system was implemented.

The report was a reflection on the decline in fortune for the town, with especially the traders of the High Street beginning to feel the failure of the London Corn Market. After 1873 bad harvests and disease amongst cattle were exacerbated by the effects of Free Trade, whereby foreign corn, cheap meat and dairy produce flooded the market. Many landowners, including the Coopers, faced financial losses and were forced to sell parts, if not all, of their estates.

With the railway station at Boxmoor, transport remained an important issue and further adversely affected the prosperity of the town. Consequently, the opening of a new railway line and the Midland station on 16 July 1877 was attended by the Bailiff Philip Evilthrift and the Jury. The Midland Railway line initially went to the north of Harpenden, to Chiltern Green, but after 1877 the final section was diverted into Harpenden to provide an alternative service for the travellers from Hemel Hempstead. It was a longer route to London, but saved the slow journey by the horse-drawn bus, later replaced by a motor bus in 1910, from the posting house to Boxmoor station.

A bridge was built across Marlowes in 1905, to carry the new railway to Heath Park Halt. A further short section of line was laid in the form of sidings with a passing loop, between Heath Park and Cotterells. This was replaced in 1963 with the construction of the new

Leighton Buzzard Road. A short track also went across Box Moor to supply coal for the gas works at Boxmoor, but was closed on 6 July 1958. The remains of the railway embankment can still be seen on the Moor at Two Waters.

OLD TOWN HALL, HIGH STREET 2005
H255714k (Peter Grainger)

To celebrate the new railway, the Bailiff and the Jury gave a banquet at the Town Hall, now called the Old Town Hall.

The line was noted for its steep gradients, which led to the nickname of 'Puffing Annie' for the engine, and even today local people recall the railway, known as the 'Nickey Line', with affection. Theories abound on the origin of the name, including a derivation from the knickerbockers worn by the navvies who built the railway. The new railway led to the area around Alexandra Road, the land sold by the Coopers, being developed into what was known as the 'New Town'. The name unwittingly foreshadowed the fate of the town in the following century.

Although photographs show a busy town, poverty in the slums prevailed, especially in the yards where the decline of the straw plait industry meant that women and children no longer contributed to the family income. Yet the Bailiwick at times of public celebrations, such as Queen Victoria's Golden and Diamond Jubilees, and with the help of public donations, never forgot the poor, usually in the form of a dinner. However people's generosity did not appear to extend to the 220 unfortunate inmates of the Workhouse. Built in 1836, the Workhouse stood on the old Redbourn Road, now Allandale. By the Second World War it became St Paul's Hospital and was the main maternity unit for a number of years, until transferred to the extended West Herts Hospital in 1987.

The building has since been demolished and replaced with housing.

The 19th century closed with an important event in the history of our town. In 1896 the Bailiwick petitioned the Privy Council for a Charter of Incorporation and Queen Victoria granted Hemel Hempstead its charter on 8 June 1898. It is from this charter that the present local authority derives its modern status and powers. By the charter Queen Victoria established a new Corporation known as the Mayor, Aldermen and Burgesses of Hemel Hempstead. It was ordained that the Mayor could also use the title of Bailiff. The Bailiwick tactfully elected Sir Astley Paston Cooper as the first Mayor of the newly formed Borough, and a great civic celebration was planned with Sir Astley opening Gadebridge Park to the public for the celebrations and sporting events.

HEMEL HEMPSTEAD c1960 H255037

The Post Office was listed in Kelly's Directory in 1882 as being in Alexandra Road. It was then relocated to a new site in Marlowes in 1937, and the Fire Station was moved to the vacated premises in Alexandra Road. The post office building survived until 1985 when it was replaced with a new glass structure.

CHAPTER FOUR

HEMEL HEMPSTEAD AS A NEW TOWN

THE 20TH CENTURY opened with the High Street, as the town centre, looking very much as we still know it today. In 1914 there were 98 registered businesses there, including the licensed premises. By this time the Bell and the King's Arms were hotels catering for commercial travellers. There were several bakers, and grocers, such as Chennels and the International Tea Company, that survived well into the 1960s. The Keen family continued as butchers in the High Street, with six of their shops listed in Trade Directories in 1914 and four listed in 1933; they were still in business in the 1970s.

Meanwhile, the success of the mills led to the development of Apsley, with shops and pubs becoming established along the London Road. Durrants Hill and Winifred Road were among many streets to be developed, and it was hoped that Hemel Hempstead's new sewerage system would help to eradicate outbreaks of diseases. Weymouth Street was one of the first to get new sewers in 1898. St Mary's Church was built in Apsley End in 1871, thanks to the generosity of Charles Longman and his fellow directors at John Dickinson. (The church now faces Sainsbury's). At Boxmoor village, new houses were being built in Kingsland Road and Horsecroft Road, which benefited from proximity to Boxmoor Station.

THE HOME AND COLONIAL STORES 1902 ZZZ03349 (Dacorum Heritage Trust Ltd)

The staff of the Home and Colonial Stores at 35 High Street, before the shop moved to No 23.

*Founded
in the Reign of King William IV.*

GEORGE ROLPH
LTD.

*High-Class Drapers
Outfitters and House
Furnishers*

Motor Deliveries in all
Districts

85, 87 & 89 High Street
HEMEL HEMPSTEAD

Telephone: BOXMOOR 70

GEORGE ROLPH LTD ZZZ04380
(Reproduced by courtesy of Dacorum Heritage Trust)

George Rolph was one of several department stores that traded in the High Street.

ST MARY'S CHURCH, APSLEY END 2005
H255715k (Peter Grainger)

The effects of two World Wars on Hemel Hempstead cannot be overlooked. During the First World War Hemel Hempstead was the base for the Royal Artillery. The 5th Company of the London Brigade was based in Gadebridge Park, with its headquarters in the Town Hall. By 1917 the troops had left and the camp in Gadebridge Park was converted into a military hospital.

At Dickinson's men were encouraged to enlist, and women were taken on to replace them. Apsley Mills came under the technical control of the Ministry of Munitions and Nash Mills made mortar bombs and small shells. Papermaking supplies grew scarce due to U-boat blockade and pulp was rationed. With food shortages the inhabitants of Hemel Hempstead had a struggle to survive. Before the introduction of rationing, communal kitchens were opened for the poorer families; the one in the Corn Exchange was well organised, but the other, in Apsley, caused constant concern at council meetings.

ST MARY'S CHURCH c1955 H255008

In the north aisle of St Mary's Church there is a window of two lights in memory of Lieutenants Julian and Cecil Smeathman, the sons of Lovel Smeathman, who was first Town Clerk and first freeman of the newly formed Borough of Hemel Hempstead. When the youngest son, Cecil, was wounded on 21 October 1914, his parents were informed that he was in hospital at Bailleul, just south of Ypres. A few days later, on 31 October, the Smeathmans were at the Town Hall attending a committee meeting for the relief of Belgian refugees when they received a telegram announcing Cecil's death. Within the next half hour they received another telegram informing them of Julian's death. He was killed at the front in the first battle at Ypres. It was the Smeathman's surviving son, Lt-Colonel L E Smeathman, who unveiled the War Memorial at Moor End on 26 June 1921.

After the Armistice on 11 November 1918, the Market Square was the centre of the celebrations with a thanksgiving service in St Mary's Church. A plaque in memory of the local men was erected on the wall of the north aisle of the church.

The 20th century saw the gradual transformation of Hemel Hempstead from a basically market town to one where industry predominated. At Bennets End there were a number of fields from which clay was excavated and made into bricks and tiles. This continued until the Second World War. The Kent Brush factory became established on the London Road, Apsley, and the British Paper Company flourished at Frogmore Mills. In 1933, Brock's Fireworks factory moved from London to Cupid Green; the site is now part of Woodhall Farm, a housing estate. From the beds of the Rivers Gade and Bulbourne about one sixth of the total output of watercress in the country was grown, an industry that survived until the building of the New Town. With the lack of planning restrictions, local industries became established throughout the town. Marlowes, for example, was a jumble of housing, shops, and industry, and Bank Court now stands on the site once taken by Bailey's Iron Foundry.

John Dickinson's reached its peak in the years before the Second World War. In 1935 the new card department building was erected followed by the new envelope department in 1937. Over 5,000 workers would converge daily on the mill by bus, cycle, on foot and by train (when Apsley Station was opened from 28 September 1938). Only the managerial staff could afford cars. The Guildhouse was built in 1920 as a canteen for workers, but it was also used for socials, dances and concerts. John Dickinson's had its own fire service and band. The Dickinson Apsley Band was founded in 1894 and won many awards and cups at contests, with broadcasts on the BBC between the wars. Shendish Estate, with Shendish House built in 1854, was once the home of Charles Longman, and when he died, the company made it the John Dickinson Sports Centre.

BANK COURT c1960 H255029

The High Street as town centre: Woolworths, the second shop from the right, arrived in 1937, Boots the Chemist, came in 1929 at No 39, and W H Smith was established as early as 1912, at No 38.

HIGH STREET c1955 H255006

This coal merchant once occupied a shop facing the Market Place, now St Mary's Close. The site is currently occupied by the Dacorum Volunteer Bureau, whilst the Dacorum Council for Voluntary Service is situated at the corner, at No 48.

Apart from the traders' families, usually living above their shops in the High Street, and some in private housing, the Borough Council minutes for 1927-28 reveal that there was little, if any, improvement in conditions in the High Street from the previous century. It is difficult to believe that the row of houses, Nos 66-106, were once part of an 'Insanitary Area' in 1928. Backing onto Keen's Yard they were inspected and condemned by the council. The dwellings were variously let to labourers, carpenters, and a coal merchant. After certain repairs had been carried out, a common lodging house at No 74 and the Brewers Arms at Nos 76-78 were allowed to continue in business, with the Brewers Arms trading until the mid 1950s. The other houses were ordered to be repaired and several improvements were carried out. Nos 82 and 84 were rebuilt but Nos 102-106 were demolished.

Keen's Yard, now a well-landscaped car park constructed by the council in 1979, and extended in 1982, not only had 11 dilapidated cottages, but also two slaughter houses and several yards with pigs and manure. It was not until 29 May 1930 that the council resolved that the area should be demolished under a clearance scheme. This was the council's response to the government's 'Slum Clearance Scheme'. The owners of the 24 dwellings in Cherry Bounce also had demolition orders served on them. The accommodation in the yards and courts off the High Street were also declared unfit for habitation and by September 1933 all the condemned properties were finally demolished.

The council built 42 houses in Chapel Street and Sun Meadow, now Sunmead Road, and 32 houses were constructed on a site at Hand Post Farm, near the present Queensway. On 29 November 1932 the Borough Treasurer, reported to the committee that 282 people had been re-housed. Later, the council also built an estate at Beechfield Road, Boxmoor, where once there were only cornfields.

With the threat of war looming on the horizon the borough council turned its attention to the organisation of local defence and preliminary preparations for war. As early as 1935, local councils were required by the Home Office to review the arrangements for air raid precautions (ARP). By June 1937 Hemel Hempstead had established several able committees to deal with these matters. Gas masks were being assembled at Apsley Mills and overtime was being worked to make boxes and carriers for gas masks. As from Friday, 1 September 1939, the town was ready to receive the first evacuees from London. War was formally declared on Sunday 3 September 1939.

Hemel Hempstead schools were organised to receive the evacuees. A report by the chairman of Hemel Hempstead Education Committee stated that 1,083 children together with 88 teachers and another 291 'unattached' evacuees' from London were attending borough schools.

One local lady, Vera Dormer (née Stone), recalls that in 1939 she attended Crabtree Lane Girls School. Vera remembers the intake of evacuees was so large that, as in other local schools, the 'double shift' system was introduced. The local children attended in the morning and the evacuees in the afternoon. This double shift system proved unsatisfactory, so the education committee ultimately found accommodation in church halls, tennis clubs and even club huts, so that local children and evacuees could receive full time education. Vera recalls being taught some of the time at her school and spending the afternoons in a draughty Methodist church hall.

On the industrial front there was a large intake of women at Dickinson's to be trained for war work and both day and night shifts were worked. Dickinson's produced an enormous amount of war material including engineering products, paper-based items and moulded plastics for aircraft parts. Apsley Mills, for example, produced 3,000 tons of 'window mixture'. This mixture of paper and foil strips was dropped by aircraft to confuse enemy radar. The production of fireworks continued at Brock's, but now the varieties became specialised signal rockets and parachute flares. Kent's continued to manufacture brushes but some hairbrushes were special models. They were made so that the back could be removed and the cavity used to conceal material to aid prisoners of war to escape.

THE LOWER END OF MARLOWES c1947 ZZZ03360 (Dacorum Heritage Trust Ltd)

This photograph was taken looking towards the bridge, where the houses were slums. The shops lining the pavement are where Marks & Spencer now stands.

Apart from a number of bombs falling in Gadebridge Park, no damage was done to the High Street. However, nine people were killed when bombs fell in Belswains Lane, Nash Mills, on the night of 10/11 May 1941. The dead included a child and two ARP wardens. Two houses were destroyed and other houses nearby had their ceilings collapse and doors and windows blown in. Nash Mills School and the Methodist Chapel were also severely damaged.

In 1940 the Home Guard established its HQ at 47 High Street, and Gadebridge Park was used for manoeuvres. Later, the Home Guard moved to the Drill Hall, which once stood in Bury Road, leaving 47 High Street as the Food Office. Councillor Derek Townsend remembers that this was the office that issued ration books, cod liver oil tablets and rosehip syrup. Derek, who lived with his family in one of the large cottages in Half Moon Yard, where the day centre for the elderly now stands, was one of the children who enjoyed a street party given by James Bollino, a greengrocer at No 74, to celebrate VE (Victory in Europe) Day, 1945. Derek grew up to become Mayor of Dacorum 2001/02.

The Box Moor Trust gave a party on the moor for the children of Boxmoor and street parties took place throughout the town. A day's paid leave was granted to employees at Dickinson's to celebrate both VE and VJ (Victory in Japan) Days.

The most dramatic change in Hemel Hempstead was a direct result of the Second World War. It is indeed possible that if Hemel Hempstead had not been classified as a New Town, it could have ended up as a backwater facing possible ruin. The streets, pavements and most of the buildings were in a bad state. The town centre and the High Street showed signs of decay with St Mary's Church surrounded by an overgrown and neglected churchyard. By the mid 20th century Hemel Hempstead, once a prosperous market town, had stagnated. But no celebrations took place for the plan to create a New Town, for it was an unpopular decision with local people.

Nationally, one of the most urgent post-war problems was the crisis of the homeless caused by the bombing of major cities, particularly London. Before the Second World War, rehabilitation of depressed areas and relocation of industry had begun in a slow way, but discussion of the problem continued during the war. A strategy evolved to identify Development Areas.

In the Abercrombie, or Greater London Plan, published in 1944, it was proposed that several satellite towns should be built around London. Industry and people would then be encouraged to move out of London to these New Towns, with the reduction of the population of London by a million. The towns were to be designed to attract all classes of the community and they were planned to provide jobs as well as homes for their citizens so they should not merely be dormitory suburbs.

Redbourn was one of the selected sites, but was considered to be too close to St Albans; in addition one third of the proposed site was in the Borough of Hemel Hempstead. Sir Patrick Abercrombie, in his report on local towns, had stated that Hemel Hempstead was unsuitable for a New Town because of its steep hills. However, the New Town Committee, created in 1945, produced another report, and the Minister of Town and Country Planning, Mr Silkin (later Lord Silkin), announced in July 1946, that Hemel Hempstead had been selected to be a New Town.

Fact File

A leader in The Hemel Hempstead, 10 May 1946, strongly criticized any suggestion for the town's development. The editor claimed that the wartime evacuation had shown that the London way of life was not that of Hemel Hempstead. How many ' undesirables' were likely to be among the 30,000 Londoners who would want to come to the town?

But was Hemel Hempstead really the attractive town that The Gazette and the citizens of Hemel Hempstead so desperately wanted left unchanged? In his Report, Sir Patrick Abercrombie had levelled strong criticism against Hemel Hempstead, which was described as a 'scattered market town'. The A41 road, the railway and the canal all by-passed the town and Sir Patrick concluded that this had led to the town sprawling over the hillsides. The town was pronounced to be predominately working class, and where development occurred it was all too often cheap and untidy. Available industrial land was considered relatively inaccessible and much of the Gade Valley was derelict. Industries such as Dickinson's paper mills and Brock's fireworks employed a large percentage of women and juveniles so consequently there

THE SHOPPING PARADE, WARNERS END c1965 H255064

was insufficient work for men. The Report recommended that Hemel Hempstead was not a town to be developed any further.

Mr Silkin and the New Town Committee, however, stood by their decision that Hemel Hempstead should be developed. On 19 November 1946 the residents of Hemel Hempstead registered their protests to Mr Silkin at Apsley Guild House. But by July 1947, a High Court judgment ruled in favour of the Minister.

Nathaniel Micklem KC was one of the fiercest critics of the New Town and his Northridge Estate was later acquired by the Development Corporation to make way for houses and shops at Warners End. The grounds are now a park and Northridge Way was named after the estate.

The Development Corporation, which was formed in 1947 to build the New Town, was instructed to increase the size of Hemel Hempstead from 20,000 people

HEMEL HEMPSTEAD BUILDING SOCIETY

Cambridge House, 43 Marlowes, Hemel Hempstead
(Tel. Boxmoor 443)

Manager & Secretary : F. LINFORD, F.C.C.S.

MORTGAGES

GENEROUS ADVANCES

SPEEDY SERVICE

LOW INSPECTION
CHARGES

ADVERTISEMENT FOR HEMEL HEMPSTEAD BUILDING SOCIETY ZZZ04382 (Author's collection)

The society was one of the many businesses and organisations to officially object to the New Town.

to 60,000, with provision for industry and housing. After much criticism of the Master Plan, a modified plan was approved in 1951, by which residential areas were to be developed as neighbourhoods, each with its own shops, schools, churches, pubs and community and health centres.

ST GEORGES CHURCH, CHAULDEN c1965 H255082

THE TOP OF THE WORLD, WARNERS END c1965 H255080

CAVENDISH SCHOOL, WARNERS END c1965 H255095

Within two years 1,000 houses were built, and by 1954 an average of ten new residents were moving into Hemel Hempstead every day. Finally, 17,000 new homes were provided for people moving out of London, as the population of Hemel Hempstead increased to 70,000 by 1973. The Development Corporation's own architects designed over 130 different types of houses and flats. The new homes ranged from small terraced houses, three-bedroom semi-detached houses and four-bedroom houses.

BOXTED ROAD, WARNERS END c1965 H255069

LONG CHAULDEN c1965 H255065

Seven new neighbourhoods were finally completed: Adeyfield, Bennets End, Chaulden, Warners End, Gadebridge, Highfield and Grove Hill. Unlike these neighbourhoods, however, Leverstock Green was an existing rural village community, and care was taken to try to retain its village character. The biggest change came with the development of large residential estates as part of the New Town. A village centre was also added, with new shops, a library and a community centre.

When planning the New Town, the Development Corporation took care to preserve open spaces between the neighbourhoods. Many are playing fields, such as Reith Fields, at Adeyfield, but others are parks, such as Northridge Park and Margaret Lloyd Park at Grovehill.

Marlowes was selected to be the main shopping area. At a public inquiry on 29 November 1949 the borough council and the traders of the High Street strongly opposed

CAVENDISH SCHOOL, WARNERS END c1965 H255070

This green valley, where several football clubs play, stretches for a mile between Warners End Road and Gadebridge. Trees have now grown up in front of Cavendish School.

the decision. They proposed that the High Street should remain the town centre and should be extended. However, they were overruled in favour of the Development Corporation plan. The west side of Marlowes and all the roads and buildings as far as Cotterills were demolished, with only the post office and the Methodist Church remaining. A row of shops, built in the 1930s and known as the Parade, the Carey Baptist Church, and a few houses were the only premises to survive on the east side. Shops, such as the Flower Box and Humphreys, the corn merchant, managed to continue trading by relocating to the Old Town.

The isolation of the High Street started with the transfer of the town's bus terminal from Bury Road to a temporary site opposite Hillfield Road, Marlowes, in October 1953. The move was necessary because of the construction of Queensway and road works in connection with the New Town Centre. A new bus terminal to serve Marlowes shopping centre was not built for another two years,

Fact File

People arriving in Hemel Hempstead, when the New Town was first built, must have been confused to find that the telephone exchange was Boxmoor, and the railway station was called Boxmoor Station. No doubt they concluded that it was all part of strange country ways. It was not until 1963 that the telephone exchange was renamed Hemel Hempstead, and in 1965 that the station was rebuilt and renamed Hemel Hempstead.

but it foreshadowed the fate of the High Street as the latter was left with only a two-hourly bus service from Great Gaddesden and a reduced service from Adeyfield.

In 1956 Woolworths, Boots, and W H Smith were amongst the first of the multiples to move to new premises in Marlowes, and when the market was relocated to Marlowes in August 1955, the local traders' fears for the High Street became a reality.

By March 1963 166 new shops were completed and occupied, with others under construction. The shops, offices and banks were designed by some of the foremost architects of the day. Bank Court was an attractive feature but its fountain was later removed.

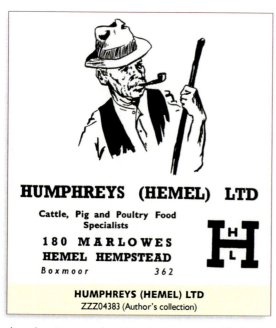

HUMPHREYS (HEMEL) LTD

Cattle, Pig and Poultry Food
Specialists

180 MARLOWES
HEMEL HEMPSTEAD

Boxmoor   362

HUMPHREYS (HEMEL) LTD
ZZZ04383 (Author's collection)

An advertisement for Humphreys at their Marlowes address.

MARLOWES c1965   H255046

THE TOWN CENTRE c1960 H255027

The borough council too, played its part in the development of the town, with the building of a civic centre and the Pavilion. A public library, and a college of further education were added by the county council. In 1958 the police station was moved from Bury Mill End (now the corner of Warners End Road) to Combe Street. The fire station in Alexandra Road proved insufficient for modern day needs, and in 1969 a new fire station opened in Queensway.

Of course, things sometimes went wrong and not everyone was happy. The Rainbow, now sited in Marlowes, is meant to represent Hemel Hempstead as the fulfillment of peoples' dreams. But many Londoners found it difficult to adjust to living in a New Town and suffered from what became known as the 'New Town Blues'. The local residents, on the other hand, resented the newcomers. Fred and Mary Smith, for example, recall that local people were not eligible for the new houses, and how they envied the newcomers living in modern houses whilst they had to start married life in an old property without 'mod cons'. Many residents also had to leave their homes and felt that the compensation paid was inadequate. Farmers in particular came off badly, as 3,500 acres of farmland was compulsorily purchased to make way for the New Town.

CIVIC CENTRE, MARLOWES 2005 H255716k (Peter Grainger)

THE PAVILION c1965 H255150

The Pavilion was officially opened in 1966. Across Combe Street stands the Odeon Cinema, opened in August 1960, to replace the old Luxor cinema, which had been demolished to make way for Woolworths. The Odeon later became a bingo hall and it has now been converted into a pub.

Opening attractions at the Pavilion included big band concerts, symphony concerts, professional wrestling, and Saturday night dances. The annual Mayor's Banquet was the most prestigious event, and as the Pavilion was also available for private hire, most of the town's functions were held there.

The course of the River Gade was altered to provide an all-important focal point, the attractive Water Gardens designed by

SUPPER DANCES AT THE PAVILION
ZZZ04384 (Author's collection)

Later, supper dances gave way to discos and pop groups.

Sir G A Jellicoe. The plans originally included two helicopter pads, one at each end of the Water Gardens, but these never materialised. The River Gade leaves the Water Gardens and flows through the Plough Roundabout, (named after the demolished Plough public house), built as part of a large scheme of road improvements at the approach of Marlowes. The dated Heath Park Hotel was replaced by a modern pub, and this, in turn, was demolished to provide a site for flats. The War Memorial, which once stood at Moor End, was moved to a more attractive place, next to St John's Church.

Fact File

The Plough Roundabout was changed in 1973 to a circular road with traffic moving in both directions and mini-roundabouts at each junction. It is known locally as the 'magic roundabout' and is one of Hemel Hempstead's claims to fame.

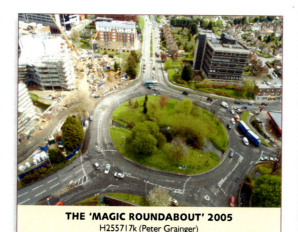

THE 'MAGIC ROUNDABOUT' 2005
H255717k (Peter Grainger)

THE ROCK AND ROLL STATUES AND WATER GARDENS c1960 H255041

SHELL MEX BUILDINGS AND GARDENS c1965 H255050

The Hemel Hempstead to Harpenden railway line was closed in 1959. Although the bridge which spanned the entrance to Marlowes was dirty and shabby, over 500 people watched it being demolished at midnight on 6 July 1960. The Shell Mex buildings (BP House) then replaced the bridge at the entrance to the town, but was closed in 1983 due to structural problems and later demolished.

The industrial area, known as Maylands Avenue, was constructed to the south-east of the town. The increase in population and industrial and commercial development brought huge economic gains to the area. Household names such as Kodak, Crossfields and Dixons were supported by other large and many smaller companies that all made valuable contributions to the town. Junction 8 of the M1 Motorway is immediately adjacent to the main industrial area and BP built prestigious offices at the entrance to Hemel Hempstead. With the industrial revolution of the 1980s declining industries were superceded by the newest hi-tech companies.

DIXONS, MAYLANDS AVENUE 2005
H255718k (Peter Grainger)

KODAK HOUSE 2005 H255719k (Peter Grainger)

The 18-storey Kodak House was built in 1971. As one of the town's major employers, Kodak gave £10,000 for a new children's playground to be built in Gadebridge Park to replace the one lost by the construction of the Plough roundabout. Kodak are now considering turning the photographic giant into a digital company. Plans have already gone ahead to sell Kodak House and to move its HQ to Harrow, with 300 members of staff relocated. A further 350 people will be moved to other Hemel Hempstead offices.

On 1 April 1962 under the provision of the New Towns Act 1959, the assets of the Development Corporation were taken over by the Commission for the New Town. Finally the housing was transferred to the local authority in 1978, but community assets such as car parks and the Water Gardens, which should have followed, were not transferred until the early 1990s. When local government reorganisation took place in 1974 the seat of the new Dacorum District Council was naturally in Hemel Hempstead.

In addition to the Development Corporation and local authority housing, private development was also of importance. Then when the 'Right to Buy' scheme came into being, many tenants purchased their homes. A lot of people consequently established 'roots' in the area and have retired here. Second and third generations have established close-knit communities.

By the 1980s, the market and the linear shopping area in Marlowes were dated and losing trade. The council, after wide public consultation, improved the town centre with a refurbished market and the pedestrianisation of Marlowes. A new shopping mall was added, and this together with out-of-town supermarkets and a Leisure World all contributed to Hemel Hempstead's growing prosperity. The council also refurbished and modernised the neighbourhood shopping centres.

97

MARLOWES SHOPPING CENTRE 2005 H255721k (Peter Grainger)

MARLOWES 2005 H255720k (Peter Grainger)

Marlowes after pedestrianisation.

MARLOWES SHOPPING CENTRE 2005
H255721k (Peter Grainger)

On the other hand, the Development Corporation's 1956-57 report to the government expressed grave concern for the future role of the High Street. With the relocation of the market, the big multiple stores to Marlowes, and the banks to Bank Court, the High Street was gradually being abandoned. Finally, in 1966, the council offices moved from the Town Hall to the new Civic Centre. By the mid 1960s the High Street began to show unmistakable signs of decay. In 1968, Hemel Hempstead Borough

Council, the Commission for New Towns, the Civic Trust and the High Street Association promoted a street improvement scheme, and over the years the High Street has been cleaned and restored. The Old Town Hall was repaired and transformed into an Arts Centre, the old market square was rebuilt and the once shabby alleys and corner sites were improved beyond recognition. The churchyard was cleared and the gravestones relocated to make way for a garden.

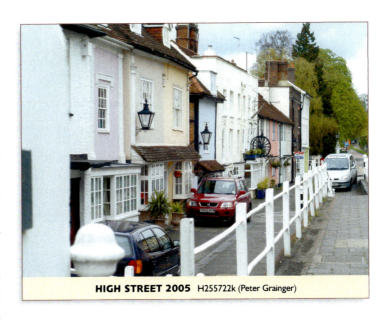

HIGH STREET 2005 H255722k (Peter Grainger)

With very few exceptions the owners and tenants redecorated and repaired their properties. Many businesses were transformed into private houses and attractive housing developments have taken place around the High Street. The council subsequently renamed the whole area as the Old Town Centre.

In 1984 Dacorum District Council, under the leadership of Councillor John Buteux, successfully petitioned the queen and borough status was awarded in May 1986. Each element of the Arms represents a part of the borough. The Tudor rose in the centre marks the connection of Hemel Hempstead with Henry VIII, and the seven oak leaves surrounding the rose represent the districts amalgamated into the borough. The stags are the insignia of Tring, and the crown in the crest is a reference to Berkhamsted Castle.

As Hemel Hempstead moved towards the close of the 20th century, a new important chapter in the history of the town was about to be written.

THE COAT OF ARMS, DACORUM BOROUGH COUNCIL
ZZZ04385 (Reproduced by kind permission of the Chief Executive, Dacorum Borough Council)

This coat of arms was designed by Peter Grainger.

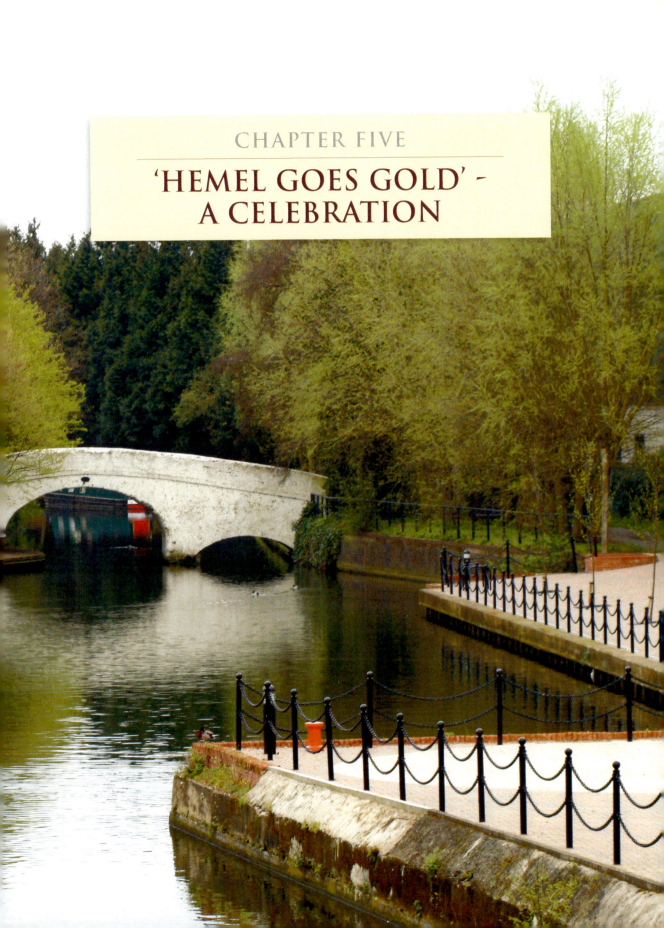

CHAPTER FIVE

'HEMEL GOES GOLD' – A CELEBRATION

IN 1997, Dacorum Borough Council announced a celebration of Hemel Hempstead New Town's 50th birthday, under the banner, 'Hemel Goes Gold'. As October 1947 marked the first public exhibition of the plans for Hemel Hempstead's role as a New Town, the council expressed the wish that September and October 1997 would be a time of public celebration. Unfortunately the opening extravaganza in the town centre had to be cancelled because of the funeral of Princess Diana.

Few people could deny the economic prosperity the New Town had brought to Hemel Hempstead, and indeed, the town had become such a cohesive society that many local children and even adults appeared to be unaware that they were living in a New Town. The Dacorum Heritage Trust, therefore, staged a special New Town Touring Exhibition, and a storyteller together with a musician visited local schools to help the pupils create songs and music on the Hemel Goes Gold theme.

The people of Hemel Hempstead also celebrated the millennium year with community parties and street parties.

On 10 September, there was a special service at St Mary's Church, which also feted the 850th anniversary of the church. A new stained glass window to commemorate the millennium was dedicated and installed at the south-west end of the church. The glass artist, Jane Campbell, has produced a lively and contemporary abstract design that brings warmth and light into the church.

Among many other events held in the town was the setting up of a time capsule designed to be used as a children's seat, which was installed at Thumpers, Highfield. Funded partly by the borough council and the residents of Thumpers, the capsule contains all the hopes and dreams for the area. In July 2000 the council arranged a further excavation of the Roman villa in Gadebridge Park. Once again, Dr David Neal headed the dig watched by large crowds of the public.

The shopping centre at Adeyfield is named after Queen Elizabeth II. Queensway was so named because that was the route Her Majesty travelled before turning into Alexandra Road, to visit Adeyfield in 1952.

Great celebrations took place to mark the Queen's Golden Jubilee, for it was also the golden celebration of Queen Elizabeth II's visit to the town 50 years ago. To commemorate the visit of Her Majesty to lay the foundation stone of St Barnabas Church,

Fact File

The highlight of the celebrations was a packed Pavilion, with an audience of 800, to watch a collection of old movie films from the town's past. The projectionist for the night was Alan Willmott, who was once the projectionist at the Princess cinema, which was demolished to make way for the civic centre. Helping Alan was Tony Rogers from the old Luxor cinema.

QUEEN'S SQUARE c1960 H255018

Adeyfield, on 20 July 1952, the Adeyfield Neighbourhood Association organised a Jubilee Fair on 20 July 2002, on Reith Field. The event brought together the community, schools, churches and residents to stage an exhibition of the Queen's visit. The Mayor of Dacorum, Councillor Catherine Appleby, was greeted by the association's president, Hon Alderman Les Tabor, after which she opened the fair. Over 3,000 people enjoyed the charity stalls, sideshows, and the arena displays. In addition, a special exhibition of photographs was staged by Michael Stanyon in St Barnabas Church.

One of the members playing in the Hemel Hempstead Band that day was Peter Davis, who also played in the Dickinson Band, 50 years previously, for the Queen. Special guests included people who, as children, had been selected to be presented to the Queen.

LORNA HUMPHRIES AND LESTER [
ADEYFIELD 1952 ZZZ04386 (Reproduced

...RD PRESENTING A BOUQUET TO THE QUEEN,
...y of Dacorum Borough Council Archives, photographer unknown)

In 1952 Lorna West, née Humphries, was chosen to present a bouquet of flowers to the Queen, with Lester Pritchard. The fathers of the two five-year-old children were the wardens of the new church. Lorna recalls that the day was quite magical and how thrilled she was when she accidentally touched the Queen's gloved hand. Beverly Davis, née Adams, also tells how her family was presented to the Queen. As her parents were the first tenants of the New Town in 1950, the Queen visited their home. The Queen also met the Neals, the third family to move to the New Town (see fact file box, below).

Fact File

The little boy who told the Queen how much his family liked their new surroundings grew up to become the archaeologist Dr David Neal. One of the anecdotes that David tells is how, three weeks prior to the Queen's visit, officials from the Development Corporation arrived to teach the children the correct way to bow and curtsey.

But what does the future hold for Hemel Hempstead as it now approaches its Diamond Jubilee as a New Town? Our town has always been one with a history of change, and the former Dickinson Apsley site, which was once the centre of a vast world-wide paper making enterprise, is now replaced by large retail stores and housing.

NASH MILLS 2005 H255723k (Peter Grainger)

The new development on the former John Dickinson site.

Industry at Nash Mills has now disappeared to become a new housing development. Frogmore Mill, together with The Cottage, extended in 1927 to become the new boardroom for Apsley Mill, has survived to be transformed into a new venture, the Apsley Paper Trail. In 2002, Dacorum Borough Council bought Frogmore Mill and leased it to the directors of the Paper Trail. It is hoped that this will become a tourist attraction to include a working mill, and exhibition areas. The Dacorum Heritage Trust, which now has museum status, is working with the directors of the Paper Trail, and has already staged several exhibitions at Frogmore Mill.

However, a change all the citizens of the town are united to oppose is the proposed reduction of services available at Hemel Hempstead General Hospital. The arguments continue, with the opposition led by Mrs Zena Bulmore. No one knows for certain what the outcome will be, but the Special Baby Care Unit has recently been moved to Watford Hospital.

The departure of several big-name businesses including Dickinson's, Kodak, Dexion and Dupont is sad but already several new firms, such as Isa, are arriving and many new factories are under construction. The Council have plans to regenerate Maylands Avenue, and new signs, a website and improved roundabouts are some of the projects already in hand.

ISA, MAYLANDS AVENUE 2005 H255724k (Peter Grainger)

THE ENTRANCE TO MARLOWES AND THE GARDENS c1960 H255049

After the BP building was demolished the site was boarded up. Alternative routes then gave access to the town centre.

The council welcomes the Riverside development because of the expected £55 million that will be spent every year in Hemel Hempstead, giving a much-needed boost to the local economy. The council also has plans to redevelop the Civic Zone. That development would involve building on a five-acre site covering the Market Square, bus station, part of Waterhouse Street and the Water Gardens car park, thus making a real feature of the River Gade and the Water Gardens. Plans also allow for a new modern library located within a Learning Zone. A new health centre and other services are also planned. The £75 million project will be paid for by offering up the site north of Combe Street to Queensway to be redeveloped into a new supermarket and housing.

The outdated Pavilion was demolished in 2002 and the council are already looking at plans to replace it with a largely self-financing Arts and Entertainment

venue. The market may be moved to the pedestrianised zone of Marlowes and it has been suggested that the Antiques Market be relocated to the High Street.

The Old Town Centre should not be

THE RIVERSIDE DEVELOPMENT 2005
H255725k (Peter Grainger)

thought of as being divorced from the New Town for it represents an asset of the utmost value for the town as a whole, by contributing a sense of historical roots and community which otherwise would be lacking. As the town centre has moved further south to Marlowes, the High Street has learnt to adapt and change with the times, even to being the setting of several television series.

Riverside, a new shopping centre, is planned to occupy the derelict site at the entrance to the town and it is hoped that it will be completed by Christmas 2005. Apart from providing a new gateway to the Town Centre, Riverside will include a full range Debenhams department store, HMV, Next and 20 other stores. Built over three stories, there will be bars, restaurants and a Premier Lodge Hotel. In addition, a 350 space multi-storey car park is being constructed, with a major new bus link for the town centre. Riverside will overlook the Water Gardens and the River Gade will flow through the centre. The site's open-air design was chosen to link up with Marlowes and Hemel's existing pedestrianised zone, to create one large shopping centre.

The Flower Box, now Enchanted Castles, at 64 High Street underwent a metamorphosis to a restaurant called 'Pie in the Sky', with Inspector Crabb as a the proprietor, during the television series of the same name, screened by the BBC in 1997. More recently, the High Street has become a setting for several episodes of ITV's 'Foyle's War', and the Old Town Centre has also starred in ITV's 'Tales from the Country'.

Every year the High Street is closed to stage a Victorian Christmas Fayre, complete with 'Queen Victoria' and a Victorian Father Christmas. The event has become a big feature of the town and it is hoped that the Farmers' Market and French Market will also become regular attractions. Indeed, as one of Dacorum Borough Council's conservation areas, the High Street is now one of the most attractive streets in Hertfordshire.

Box Moor continues to give pleasure to the residents of Hemel Hempstead, whether it be enjoying the cricket, the fairs, the annual conker festival or the many other events organised by local clubs. 'Music on the Moor', first held in the summers of 2001 and 2003, has proved so popular that it will now become a permanent feature. Thousands of people gather to enjoy a wide range of music, from popular music to classics and jazz performed by local choirs and bands. The Trustees also appreciate the importance of raising public awareness, especially in the fields of environment and education. Once an important freight-carrying commercial artery, the canal is today a place for recreational use with the narrow boats now used for holiday cruising.

HIGH STREET, THE FRENCH MARKET 2005 ZZZ04387
(Reproduced by kind permission of Maureen Parkins)

THE WATER FEATURE, MARLOWES 2005 H255726k (Peter Grainger)

GADEBRIDGE PARK 2005 H255727k (Peter Grainger)

Dacorum's Hemel Hempstead Sports Centre has fine facilities for swimming and diving. There is a fully equipped gymnasium, a large sports hall, and badminton and squash courts. At Jarman's Field is Rank Leisure World, which offers a wide range of attractions including tenpin bowling, ice skating and a 'waterworld'.

Throughout the town close attention has always been paid to landscaping, with the careful preservation of all possible existing trees. The town has also reaped the benefit of some 18,000 trees, 244,750 hedge plants and over 66,000 shrubs originally planted by the Development Corporation.

First started by the Development Corporation, with the famous Rock and Roll statues in the Water Gardens, major artworks have always been an important asset to the town. More recently, additional statues have been commissioned by Dacorum Borough Council and positioned throughout the length of the pedestrianised area of Marlowes. The Rainbow was unveiled by its American sculptor, Colin Lambert, in 1993. The Water Feature, sculpted by Michael Rizello OBE, celebrates youth with a bronze sculpture of three children playing in the water. In addition there is a quirky bronze relief map depicting Hemel Hempstead as it was in 1947, and a Steel Tree with each panel of the tree showing events of the town past and present.

With a population of over 80,000, Hemel Hempstead is indeed a thriving town. Well placed close to two motorways and with fast links to London by rail from Hemel Hempstead and Apsley railway stations, the town is in an ideal location for business success. Hemel Hempstead has become a fusion of new neighbourhoods, Marlowes and the Old Town, yet our town still retains its links with the past as it continues to enjoy the pleasant atmosphere of a country town.

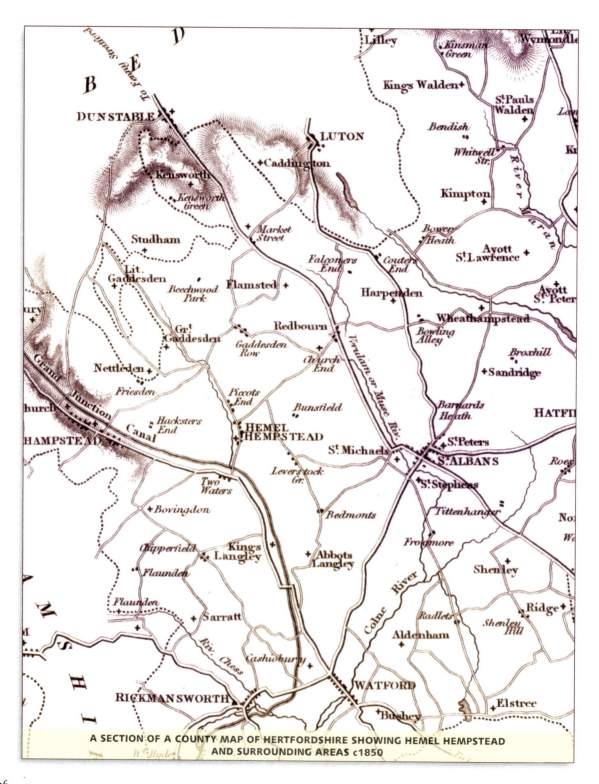

A SECTION OF A COUNTY MAP OF HERTFORDSHIRE SHOWING HEMEL HEMPSTEAD AND SURROUNDING AREAS c1850

ACKNOWLEDGEMENTS AND BIBLIOGRAPHY

ACKNOWLEDGEMENTS

I would like to thank my husband and my family for all their support during the writing of this book. My grateful thanks are due to my photographer, Peter Grainger, who is always a pleasure to work with. I would also like to acknowledge the help given by Dacorum Borough Council, the Dacorum Heritage Trust, Hemel Hempstead Movie Makers and the many local people who so kindly shared their memories of the town with me.

BIBLIOGRAPHY

P Abercrombie: The Greater London Plan, London, 1944

E Buteux: A Walk Round St Mary's Church, Hemel Hempstead, Hertfordshire, Church Press, Yorks, 2000

E Buteux: Time's Highway, Dacorum Heritage Trust, 1998

Hemel Hempstead Development Corporation: The Development of Hemel Hempstead, Hemel Hempstead, 1953

J and R Hands: Royalty to Commoners - Four Hundred Years of the Box Moor Trust, Alpine Press, Kings Langley, 2004

C Shipman and D Jackson: Dacorum - Within Living Memory, Dacorum Borough Council, Watford, 1988

A J Ward: The Early History of Paper Making, Dacorum Heritage Trust, 2003

S and G Woodward: The Nickey Line, Oakwood Press, 1996

FRITH PRODUCTS & SERVICES

Francis Frith would doubtless be pleased to know that the pioneering publishing venture he started in 1860 still continues today. Over a hundred and forty years later, The Francis Frith Collection continues in the same innovative tradition and is now one of the foremost publishers of vintage photographs in the world. Some of the current activities include:

INTERIOR DECORATION

Today Frith's photographs can be seen framed and as giant wall murals in thousands of pubs, restaurants, hotels, banks, retail stores and other public buildings throughout the country. In every case they enhance the unique local atmosphere of the places they depict and provide reminders of gentler days in an increasingly busy and frenetic world.

PRODUCT PROMOTIONS

Frith products are used by many major companies to promote the sales of their own products or to reinforce their own history and heritage. Frith promotions have been used by Hovis bread, Courage beers, Scots Porage Oats, Colman's mustard, Cadbury's foods, Mellow Birds coffee, Dunhill pipe tobacco, Guinness, and Bulmer's Cider.

GENEALOGY AND FAMILY HISTORY

As the interest in family history and roots grows world-wide, more and more people are turning to Frith's photographs of Great Britain for images of the towns, villages and streets where their ancestors lived; and, of course, photographs of the churches and chapels where their ancestors were christened, married and buried are an essential part of every genealogy tree and family album.

FRITH PRODUCTS

All Frith photographs are available Framed or just as Mounted Prints and Posters (size 23 x 16 inches). These may be ordered from the address below. Other products available are - Address Books, Calendars, Jigsaws, Canvas Prints, Postcards and local and prestige books.

THE INTERNET

Already ninety thousand Frith photographs can be viewed and purchased on the internet through the Frith websites and a myriad of partner sites.

For more detailed information on Frith products, look at this site:
www.francisfrith.com

See the complete list of Frith Books at: www.francisfrith.com
This web site is regularly updated with the latest list of publications from The Francis Frith Collection. If you wish to buy books relating to another part of the country that your local bookshop does not stock, you may purchase on-line.

For further information, trade, or author enquiries please contact us at the address below:
The Francis Frith Collection, Unit 6, Oakley Business Park, Wylye Road, Dinton, Wiltshire SP3 5EU.
Tel: +44 (0)1722 716 376 Fax: +44 (0)1722 716 881 Email: sales@francisfrith.co.uk

See Frith products on the internet at www.francisfrith.com

FREE PRINT OF YOUR CHOICE
CHOOSE A PHOTOGRAPH FROM THIS BOOK
+ £3.80 POSTAGE

Mounted Print

Overall size 14 x 11 inches (355 x 280mm)

TO RECEIVE YOUR FREE PRINT

Choose any Frith photograph in this book

Simply complete the Voucher opposite and return it with your remittance for £3.50 (to cover postage and handling) and we will print the photograph of your choice in SEPIA (size 11 x 8 inches) and supply it in a cream mount ready to frame (overall size 14 x 11 inches).

Order additional Mounted Prints
at HALF PRICE - £12.00 each (normally £24.00)

If you would like to order more Frith prints from this book, possibly as gifts for friends and family, you can buy them at half price (with no additional postage costs).

Have your Mounted Prints framed

For an extra £20.00 per print you can have your mounted print(s) framed in an elegant polished wood and gilt moulding, overall size 16 x 13 inches (no additional postage required).

IMPORTANT!

❶ Please note: aerial photographs and photographs with a reference number starting with a "Z" are not Frith photographs and cannot be supplied under this offer.

❷ Offer valid for delivery to one UK address only.

❸ These special prices are only available if you use this form to order. You must use the ORIGINAL VOUCHER on this page (no copies permitted). We can only despatch to one UK address.

❹ This offer cannot be combined with any other offer.

As a customer your name & address will be stored by Frith but not sold or rented to third parties. Your data will be used for the purpose of this promotion only.

Send completed Voucher form to:

The Francis Frith Collection,
19 Kingsmead Business Park, Gillingham,
Dorset SP8 5FB

Voucher for **FREE** and Reduced Price Frith Prints

Please do not photocopy this voucher. Only the original is valid, so please fill it in, cut it out and return it to us with your order.

Picture ref no	Page no	Qty	Mounted @ £12.00	Framed + £20.00	Total Cost £
		1	Free of charge*	£	£
			£12.00	£	£
			£12.00	£	£
			£12.00	£	£
			£12.00	£	£
			£12.00	£	£

Please allow 28 days for delivery. Offer available to one UK address only

* Post & handling		£3.80
Total Order Cost		£

Title of this book . . . .

I enclose a cheque/postal order for £ . . . .

made payable to 'The Francis Frith Collection'

OR please debit my Mastercard / Visa / Maestro card, details below

Card Number:

Issue No (Maestro only):   Valid from (Maestro):

Card Security Number: Expires:

Signature:

Name Mr/Mrs/Ms ....

Address ....

....

....

.... Postcode ....

Daytime Tel No ....

Email ....

Valid to 31/12/16

Can you help us with information about any of the Frith photographs in this book?

We are gradually compiling an historical record for each of the photographs in the Frith archive. It is always fascinating to find out the names of the people shown in the pictures, as well as insights into the shops, buildings and other features depicted.

If you recognize anyone in the photographs in this book, or if you have information not already included in the author's caption, do let us know. We would love to hear from you, and will try to publish it in future books or articles.

An Invitation from The Francis Frith Collection to Share Your Memories

The 'Share Your Memories' feature of our website allows members of the public to add personal memories relating to the places featured in our photographs, or comment on others already added. Seeing a place from your past can rekindle forgotten or long held memories. Why not visit the website, find photographs of places you know well and add YOUR story for others to read and enjoy? We would love to hear from you!

www.francisfrith.com/memories

Our production team

Frith books are produced by a small dedicated team at offices near Salisbury. Most have worked with the Frith Collection for many years. All have in common one quality: they have a passion for the Frith Collection.

Frith Books and Gifts

We have a wide range of books and gifts available on our website utilising our photographic archive, many of which can be individually personalised.

www.francisfrith.com